THE MIND AND ART OF

ALBERT JAY NOCK

THE MIND AND ART OF

ALBERT JAY NOCK

Robert M. Crunden

HENRY REGNERY COMPANY

CHICAGO 1964

To Pat

WHAT I have attempted in this book is not a conventional biography, or even a sketch of the subject. I have tried to portray a mind as it slowly discovers itself in the confrontation of the events of thirty-five years of history. Because of this aim, I have included only what I feel to be the minimum necessary details of Nock's life, and made little effort to amass pages of interesting but otherwise irrelevant material. The man who attempts to do this will have his problems: Nock was fanatical about keeping private matters private, and material of this sort is scarce indeed. I thought it only fair to rely primarily on the man's published work, since this is generally more carefully considered, and often a more accurate indicator of a man's ideas than random and unexplained side comments in letters to friends who may need little or no guidance. I have also consulted extensive manuscript material, particularly for the opening chapter, for factual matters and the like. Material obtained from interviews is scattered throughout the book.

The bibliography at the end of the book is not complete. I have omitted many books that I used only incidentally, all book reviews (these are cited in the notes), and all reprints. The bibliography does include all of the longer, unsigned articles that Nock wrote for the *Freeman*. Much evidence exists to indicate that he also wrote many of the Interpreter's House columns for *American Magazine*, and a number of editorials for the *Nation* during 1918–19, for the *New Freeman*, 1930–31, and for the *American Mercury*, 1936–39. None of these possibilities is included in the list.

The Palmer papers, including much useful material, are now

at Yale. The condition and location of the rest of the Nock papers is less definite. A large selection of correspondence, personal as well as public, totaling five typewritten volumes, is also with the Nock papers at Yale, to be opened after the death of Ruth Robinson. I have seen excerpts from these papers before they were sent to Yale and closed. Copies of some of these letters are held by Miss Robinson, the Nock brothers, and myself. I also have copies of much of the material now in the Nock papers at the Library of Congress. Most of the Library of Congress material I found of little use. Of peripheral value is a large group of clippings of book reviews, here and in England, which is also at Yale. Smith College has the Garrison papers, which include a scattering of Nock material.

I have also had much assistance from other sources. Mr. Robert Thornton placed his large collection of Nock miscellany at my disposal, and sent me copies of hard-to-find books. The Reverend Mr. Edmund Opitz introduced me to a number of valuable sources, and corrected several mistakes in checking an early draft of the manuscript. I have also interviewed personally, and received valuable information from: Dr. Samuel A. Nock, Dr. Francis J. Nock, Paul Palmer, Frank Chodorov, Ruth Robinson, B. W. Huebsch, and William Tachau. By mail, I have received extensive help from these people, and from Lewis Mumford, Richard Gummere, Jr., and Prof. Harry Elmer Barnes. I received replies to my questions from Van Wyck Brooks, William Henry Chamberlin, Mark Van Doren, Suzanne La Follette, Robert Hillyer, Jacques Barzun, John Dos Passos, Rev. Roger A. Walke, Jr., the Registrars of Berkeley Divinity School and Wesleyan University, Frances Perkins, Newton Arvin, E. H. Broadhurst, Margaret S. Grierson, Will Lissner, Phyllis Evans, Max Eastman, Geroid Tanquary Robinson, Susan J. Turner, Paul Bigelow, and James J. Martin. Both of Nock's sons, Miss Robinson, and Catherine Wilson have checked the manuscript, at one stage or another, for factual and interpretive errors. Since these four, who all knew Nock well, do not always agree even about factual matters, the final responsibility of course rests with me.

My greatest debt, however, is to the members of the faculty and the deans of Yale College. Yale is the only college in the country that I know of where a project such as this one may be undertaken by an undergraduate, and I will always be thankful that at least one institution of learning is unashamed to demand just a little more than its students can accomplish. In particular, I owe a debt to the Scholar of the House Committee, under Mr. Paul Pickrel, who made it possible to omit much of the normal routine of school life, and to whom I handed a previous draft of this work; to Messrs. John M. Blum, Richard Ruland, and Roger Bannister, for their suggestions; and most of all, to Professor Edmund S. Morgan who, far and above the call of duty, helped me greatly through all the painful early stages of writing, and whose senses of style and humor helped make enjoyable a job that might well have become tedious.

CONTENTS

[xi

JOURNEYMAN SCHOLAR, 1924–39

EPILOGUE–RETIREMENT, 1939–45

THE MIND AND ART OF

ALBERT JAY NOCK

✍ ORIGINS AND APPRENTICESHIP

For some are born to be beatified
By anguish, and by grievous penance done;
And some to furnish forth the age's pride,
And to be praised of men beneath the sun;
And some are born to stand perplexed aside
From so much sorrow—of whom I am one.
—SANTAYANA

How dreary to be somebody!
How public, like a frog
To tell your name the livelong June
To an admiring bog.
—EMILY DICKINSON

CHAPTER ONE

PORTRAIT

Because he did not fit, because his ideas were so out of style, because the things he loved were not loved by those around him, he called himself a superfluous man. Perhaps he was right; but if so, America was the loser. Sometimes he was right, sometimes not, but any country would be better for being exposed to his point of view, even if only to dismiss it. Somehow, this critic of America had the priceless ability to irritate people into thought—an ability vital to any healthy society. Perhaps he knew too much history. But his immense learning, and capacity for disinterested thought, make the journey through his mind all the more fascinating. One sometimes has the disconcerting, yet rewarding, feeling that one has come face to face with a liberal education. The feeling does not make one necessarily agree with his views. Rather, it sounds the call to battle. Rarely has the experience been so refreshing.

He was a man of seemingly monumental prejudice—unconvivial, with a shell around him which no one could penetrate. To some, he seemed a cold fish, haughty and snobbish. Perhaps his personality had too many sides. Was it unsuitable for life in America, and thus enigmatic to Americans? A monumental distaste for publicity, coupled with a disdain for the opinions of the many, made him appear reclusive. When asked about his life, he would reply with outlandish tales that some believed. Soon a legend was created, and the man showed no displeasure at its creation, and even encouraged it with a sense of delight in mystery that smacked of espionage novels. Some that knew him

3

well thought his affectations absurd, while others found them interesting, even endearing. Most had a grudging respect for a man who would never, regardless of circumstances, compromise principles or integrity. He did not like the twentieth century and was unafraid to say so. Yet he would be out of place anywhere except in some fine and private place where uncooperative people could not disturb the quiet ruminations of the mind, for the mind, above all, had primacy among those things that were good.

Perhaps Clarence Day spoke his epitaph. Thoroughly familiar with Nock's work, Day was discussing him one evening. "Poor feller!" he said, "he ain't got no place to go!"

II

Although he disclaimed knowledge of it, Albert Jay Nock was born on October 13, 1870. He had a poor memory for dates, and perhaps his total unconcern for trivia pushed the year out of his head. He knew the day only because his mother celebrated her birthday ten days earlier, and the two occasions were usually combined. The family lived in Brooklyn, but Nock was born in Scranton, Pennsylvania, the home of his mother's parents. Such was the custom in those more sentimental times.

Nock's mother was Emma Sheldon Jay. Nock remained close to her throughout her life, always affectionate and devoted. Others were less charitable toward her, and reports have it that she was next to impossible to get along with. Nock's father was Joseph Albert Nock, an Episcopal clergyman. His father in turn, while a steelmaker, was a licensed Methodist preacher. Religion seems to have been a strong family force, without being overwhelming. Nock's paternal grandparents were easterners, living first in Windsor Locks, Connecticut, then in Ramapo, New York, and finally settling on Staten Island. In all three places, the grandfather was superintendent of steelworks. His eldest son, Thomas Gill, became head of the Rome, New York, Locomotive

Works. The second son, George Franklin, was superintendent of a rolling mill for the Union Pacific Railway.

The Jays were from New York, where family rumor had them in some vague niche on the family tree of John Jay. No one was concerned enough to look the relationship up, however. Mrs. Nock's ancestors were Rochellois Protestants who arrived in America in the late 1680's. For generations, they proliferated abundantly; Mrs. Nock was one of ten. With her, however, the custom stopped, for Albert was her only child, except for a daughter lost in infancy before he was born. Nock was proud of his French ancestry, and occasionally would muse upon it as the possible source of his ingrained skepticism.

The Nocks were respectably poor; they lacked little that was necessary and had little that was not. Life was quiet, secure, settled. Their neighborhood was similar; the few rich families did not ostentatiously advertise their condition, and the poor did not starve. Brooklyn, City of Churches, was the Age of Innocence equivalent of the modern suburb, and many inhabitants commuted to Manhattan daily on the horsecar lines and the East River ferry. The Nock house was in a semi-rural area, with a large garden, fruit trees, and neighbors who indulged in such pastimes as keeping guinea fowls and raising bees. The area was cosmopolitan in composition, although the vast majority of residents were of European stock; Dutch, German, French, English, and Irish Protestant were all represented.

The only child in the minister's family, while precociously intelligent, was hardly bookish. He was strong, well-built, and rarely ill. He had a quick, even violent temper, and was easily stirred into explosions of impatience and anger. When he was finished being angry, he was always ashamed and regretful, willing to do anything to atone. Eventually, he developed a well-controlled temper and a great distaste for loss of self-control. The boy's real talents showed only on the baseball diamond, where he enjoyed no little success. As a second baseman, he was asked to join a semi-professional team, and he appears to have played for them as early as age fourteen, continuing for eleven years. He achieved an excellent record on his college baseball team, and seriously considered spending several years as a real pro. His mother, her eyes on the cloth, spiked this idea and steered her son toward higher things.

When the boy was about ten, his father was called to Alpena, Michigan, a lumber town at the head of Thunder Bay. There, the egalitarianism of Brooklyn was reinforced in the rough pioneering society. In his new home, Nock's love for Jefferson, so central to his later intellectual growth, grew strong. There the wealthy wore shirtsleeves, status was of little importance, and contact with the outside world was sporadic at best. Yet, despite this lack of outside contact, there was an amateur but thriving cultural life, transplanted by some of the new arrivals. Life there, Nock wrote, gave him "a close view of equalities which I was of course too young to appraise at their full value," but which influenced him greatly. In an atmosphere of freedom, with so little "arbitrary constraint that we hardly knew government existed," the qualities of "independence, self-respect, self-reliance, dignity, diligence," however ill-formed or not understood, grew into the young man. Few policemen were ever seen and Nock "heard of no crime being committed there" in his time. On the whole, this society "might have served pretty well as a standing advertisement for Mr. Jefferson's notion that the virtues which he regarded as distinctively American thrive best in the absence of government." Such beliefs, he felt, were at the base of the Declaration of Independence, and these beliefs became the base of his philosophy.[1]

III

Nock obtained much of his education on his own, and thought this was ideal. He lived in a house of books, and his father was willing and able to guide him whenever he asked. Nock remarked that his father rarely did anything but put knowledge in front of his son and let him do with it as he wished. Nock thus had

almost complete intellectual freedom. He learned to read by star-
ing by the hour at a newspaper clipping on his wall, and improved his vocabulary by reading the dictionary for the sheer
joy of enriched curiosity. With a little help from his father, he
learned Greek and Latin with virtually no formal instruction.
He did not attend any school at all until his teens. Indeed, he
seems to have been something of a prodigy by any of the common standards.

Two elements stood out in his recollection of his education.
First, Nock was a born skeptic.

> If today for the first time I met the Primer's statement—
>
>> In Adam's fall
>> We sinnéd all.
>
> —my first question would not be, did Adam really fall? nor would
> it be, Did we all really sin? It would not even be the previous
> question, Did Adam ever really exist? It would be the question
> previous to all these three questions, namely: How could anyone
> possibly know anything about it? Moreover, not only is this the
> case now, at the close of a rather uncommonly experienced and
> reflective old age, but even though I stretch my memory to the
> utmost I do not recall a time in all my life when I would have met
> a similar or analogous statement in any other way. I can quite be-
> lieve that at three years of age, *praemonitis quae praemonenda*, I
> would have instinctively put the same question as at thirty or
> threescore.

Further, he grew to have "a fairly explicit understanding of the
fact that ignorance exists." Plato had convinced him that attempts to change the ignorant, to enlighten them, were doubtful
ventures. As time went on, he became convinced "that Calvin's
idea of invincible ignorance had a validity which the Genevese
French lawyer did not suspect."[2]
Nock's parents concurred with their son's wish to enter college, and replaced the random method of his education by study
in a private preparatory school, aimed solely at preparation for

the classical collegiate curriculum. Colleges in the nineteenth century required their candidates to prove their ability "extempore to read, construe and parse" any Latin prose or poetry presented to them and to write "true Latin prose," as well as demonstrate their skill in "making Latin verse." Similar requirements existed for Greek. "This was exactly right, exactly as it should be." Nock's love of the classics and the old education had its roots here.

The school experiences confirmed in him certain of his already developed characteristics—love of freedom, self-reliance, and high standards—and influenced his whole outlook. The school had an atmosphere of freedom. Within work hours discipline was strict, but not unkind or unreasonable. Students were never bothered with commands "against putting beans up our noses, or subjected to any snivelling talk about being on our honour, or keeping up the credit of the dear old school, or any such odious balderdash. Nevertheless, we somehow managed to behave decently, no doubt because we had no overweening inducements to behave otherwise." In this atmosphere Nock finished his preparatory education. His faith in the self as the seeker of education, rather than in the school or the teacher as the feeder of it, remained constant throughout his life. "Abraham Flexner once remarked to me that getting an education is like getting measles; you have to go where measles is." For Nock, the individual did the going; the sole job of the school was to exist and be competent.

St. Stephen's, now Bard College, where Nock began college work in 1887, "was small, never running quite to a hundred students; it wanted no more and would take no more." The atmosphere of freedom was unchanged from that of prep school: "It would be hard to imagine a set of young men living more strictly on their own." No alumni pressure group babbled about athletics or was pressured for money; quarters were shabby, and no one forced a clean-up. The contact with faculty was purely businesslike: "The authorities had nothing to do with us in a social way; our only contact with them was in business hours and for business purposes. They were men of vast learning, great dignity, always punctiliously polite, but with no affectation of cordiality. For our part, we put up no pretense of fondness for them, but our respect, pride, admiration of them, knew no bounds. We would have fought for them like Stonewall Jackson's soldiers at the drop of a hat. . . . Our preceptors were gentlemen as well as scholars." No solicitous care about life adjustment, psycho-social problems, or class attendance. Modern psychology notwithstanding, this atmosphere produced results, for ". . . the place was permeated by a profound sense of justice. . . . Each day's work was a full day's work, union hours, but we could never say we were overtasked. In my four years there I never heard of anyone getting a word of commendation for a piece of good work, though I saw a great deal of good work, even distinguished work, being done." Here too there is the theme of self-reliance, of the student seeking education rather than education seeking the student: "We were made to understand that the burden of education was on us and no one else, least of all our instructors; they were not there to help us carry it or to praise our efforts, but to see that we shouldered it in proper style and got on with it."

St. Stephen's maintained this "grand old fortifying classical curriculum" throughout the period when Nock was a student, 1887–92. He thought it was the last institution to retain this program, except for some Jesuit institutions. A student took Greek, Latin, mathematics, logic, metaphysics, and the history of the English language. If he succeeded, he received a B.A. and was expected to leave promptly. "If, on the other hand, you were not good enough to stand the appointed strain, it was presumably a matter of God's will, and nothing could be done about it."[3]

Nock's record at St. Stephen's was spotty but, on the whole, good. He entered as a senior preparatory student on October 17, 1887, qualified as a freshman the next September, and won prizes in logic (1891) and English literature (1892). He graduated third in a class of ten, the school's enrollment during this period totaling about seventy-eight, including many preparatory students.

Nock did poorly in his first term; he took Latin, Greek, and mathematics. By the end of his first year he had pulled his total average up about eight points, to seventy-nine. In his freshman year, his grades were generally in the high eighties in Latin, in the middle eighties in Greek, and in the low eighties and seventies in mathematics—averaging eighty-four. The next year he began English history and French, pulling his over-all average for the year up to over eighty-seven. His grades over the next two years were at this level, with startling drops in declamation (34) and composition (52), and startling heights in logic (98), English literature (95), Latin, and French—the most notable parts of his school record. His other studies at St. Stephen's included moral philosophy, astronomy, Hebrew, chemistry, psychology, and Greek testament.

Nock was well aware of the faults in the classical educational system, and stated them uncompromisingly. His position was that, in spite of the defects, the system was the best that could be devised to introduce formative knowledge into educable minds. The trouble with much classical training, he wrote, was that those who administered it often did poorly and, worse, people unable to profit from it were required to suffer it. A mind could be trained in the minutiae of grammar and the mechanics of language, and yet be unable to achieve formative knowledge from the process. The ineducable "gerund grinders," as Carlyle called them, were the cause of the system's failure: "It failed, as many a good system has failed, through getting into bad hands."[4]

IV

Just exactly what Nock did between 1892, when he got his B.A. at St. Stephen's, and 1898, when he was appointed an assistant rector, remains something of a mystery. He probably played baseball for several years while pursuing his studies independently—in a fashion similar to the *vagantes* of the Middle Ages. Several sources report him as doing graduate work at Berkeley Divinity School, then in Middletown, Connecticut, where he met "Zebe" Parsons, a lifelong friend who was soon ordained into the ministry; there also he enjoyed the Rabelais society he talks of in his *Memoirs*. But most of the record is unclear.

Nock entered Berkeley in the fall of 1895, but remained there only one year and received no degree. At some time he may have studied classics as a graduate student at St. Stephen's, and been a teacher there in Latin and German; but these records are also fragmentary. In 1897, he was ordained to the ministry of the Episcopal Church and in 1898 he was called to St. James Church, Titusville, Pennsylvania, as assistant to the rector, Dr. Purdon. Shortly after his arrival Dr. Purdon died, and Nock assumed full duties on New Year's Day, 1899. He enjoyed some success in Titusville, and a later church publication reported that "Dr. Nock's ministry may be characterized by his brilliant sermons and addresses and by his deep interest in the social order." Because of his great learning, the congregation was "greatly edified." One wonders how far the tongue may be in the cheek, but the report remains. More than likely, Nock was respected for his mind, but his attempts at social leveling may well have run into opposition.[5]

While in Titusville, Nock met Agnes Grumbine (1876-1935), and the two were married on April 25, 1900. Agnes appears to have been a "fine" woman in all senses of the word; excellent in appearance, dress, and thought. She does not seem to have understood the mind of her husband very well, and he in turn hardly set a normal standard as husband and father the first few years of marriage. On February 17, a year after the marriage, Samuel A. Nock was born.

In 1904, Nock accepted a call from Christ Episcopal Church in Blacksburg, Virginia, and assumed his duties there on September 1. The next year, on May 13, Francis Jay Nock was born. Nock remained at Christ Episcopal until September 15, 1907, when he left for St. Joseph's in Detroit. He remained at St. Joseph's, his last church, until he left the active ministry late in 1909 to join the staff of the *American Magazine*.

Nock's career on the *American Magazine*, 1910–14, carried him into the active world for the first time. Because of his sense of style, he had a hand in many of the magazine's articles. He also became a close friend of many of the reformers active at the time. He was a single taxer, and the single tax group, which had included Golden Rule Jones and Tom Johnson, and later Brand Whitlock, Frederic Howe, Newton D. Baker, and Peter Witt, had him as a respected member. Indeed, he was one of the major influences on Whitlock, pressuring him to write his autobiography. Unhappy and out of his depth as mayor of Toledo, the scholarly, sensitive Whitlock needed help in administration, as well as encouragement in the writing of his memoirs, and Nock was the one who provided it, even to organizing Whitlock's office for him and disposing of pressing paper work. The book, *40 Years of It*, was run serially in the *American Magazine*, and later printed in book form with an introduction by Nock.

During this period, Nock also appears to have obtained government assignments through his friend, Secretary of State William Jennings Bryan. In four trips abroad before America entered the war, Nock visited England, and was known among liberals there; he also performed some tasks in Italy, Belgium, Russia, and Berlin, the nature of which is unknown. Always secretive, Nock never discussed his affairs with anyone, and no record of these adventures is known to survive.

He wrote regularly for the *American Magazine* through 1914, even trying his hand occasionally at fiction. Only one of his stories was ever published, however, and he soon realized that creative writing was not in his line. With the coming of the war and the end of progressivism, he went first to Europe, and then to the staff of Oswald Garrison Villard's *Nation*, a liberal antiwar journal. There he wrote extensively, and achieved a brief moment of glory when an article of his, on Samuel Gompers, was the cause of the suppression of one *Nation* issue by the professional patriots of the Wilson administration, Burleson and Lamar.

On the social side, he was extremely attractive to women, and in turn quite fond of them—if, of course, they were intelligent. He was an immaculate person, neat to the point of fastidiousness, yet inclined to wear his clothes until they were shabby. Although it is possible that he had no money for clothes, he just does not seem to have noticed the state of his clothes unless someone pointed it out to him. He wore ministerial garb until 1909, and then settled on the stiff high collared dress of the 1910–20 era. Physically, he was finely, almost beautifully constructed, with small hands and feet. He stood five feet ten inches tall, and was able to keep his excellent figure throughout his life. He had brilliant blue eyes, capable of much expression, fair skin, reddish complexion, and a mustache. His head, especially the forehead, was large, and bore an iron-gray fringe of white hair long before the rest of his hair turned white.

He detested moist air, and suffered physically in humidity. Whenever storm clouds appeared, his circulation would slow and he would have a feeling of suffocation. He also detested loud noises and crowds. He felt bad upon arising, and took an hour or more to begin functioning properly. This is not the place to speculate on the connection of body and mind, but the impression remains that many of Nock's ideas were grounded in, or at least confirmed by, his physical nature.

v

What was in many ways the high point of Nock's career began in 1920 with the foundation of the *Freeman*. With Francis Neilson, a British liberal and single taxer, Nock built a magazine that achieved the status of legend among stylists and connoisseurs of the little magazine. Here he made his reputation, met a large number of influential people, and rounded out the classical education he prized so with a thorough grounding in the liberal–radical tradition of Henry George, Herbert Spencer, and others.

A bit naïve and perhaps ill-informed in 1919, he left the *Freeman* in 1924 as a well-known and respected editor. His learning both impressed and annoyed people. " 'A diligently forgotten learning is the mother of culture,' he once remarked, but he seemed to have remembered everything," Van Wyck Brooks remembered thirty years later.[6] Others were simply irritated by a man who seemed so arrogant, and who unconcernedly sprinkled untranslated quotations in a half-dozen languages throughout his work. Nock was at least partially aware of the irritation he caused many people. "One may see from [my viewpoint] how easily the temper of individuality incurs the charge of arrogance. I have always had to face this charge; I think unjustly." His manner was the expression of how he felt, and he had no wish to change.[7]

One feeling he had throughout his life was devotion to privacy, and his mania in this area explains much of his eccentricity, although hardly excusing it. As Brooks wrote: ". . . with his testy and obstinate look of a Tintoretto doge, he might have taken for his motto, 'Hide thy life,' and he was full of surprises in consequence of this—one never knew what might turn up in his thought or speech."[8] And so he would rarely give anyone his address. It was a witticism at the *Freeman* that the only way to reach him was to place a note under a certain rock in Central Park. He told no one of his clerical past and refused to admit any part of it, even to questioners who had noticed church bulletins coming to "Rev. Albert Jay Nock." Many of his closest friends never knew he had been married or had two children. He even had the habit of sometimes storing up his outgoing mail and having it posted from another state, so that the postmark would not give away his location. All of these quirks seemed engrained in his personality equally by perversity and eccentricity, although he had his reasons: "In a society like ours, bitterly resentful of privacy, the integrity of one's personality is constantly under attack from all sides; not only under direct frontal attack, but which is worse, it is always exposed to insidious influences which will infect it and rot it down. To the individualist, the integrity thus menaced is the most precious thing on earth; and the dangers to it being what they are, they beget a corresponding extreme of sensitiveness and caution which in time becomes a sort of secondary instinct." Views like this went a long way toward explaining his excessive desires for anonymity, as well as his pure hatred for newspapers and other organs of publicity.[9]

Another explanation of his love of privacy is based on the influence of Nock's mother. Mrs. Nock, although defended by one of Nock's friends as "a character, without question full of spicy comeback," who was strict with her children but not impossible, is not remembered favorably by at least one grandchild. Samuel Nock regards "domineering" to be "a fairly mild descriptive adjective" in reference to her. One of his contemporaries, he is fond of repeating, "said that when she was a little girl" in Titusville, "there were two old bitches in town," one of whom was "old lady Nock." Whatever Mrs. Nock's influence, no one questions that her son respected her and dreaded her disapproval. When he left his wife and wished to go off on his own, he made a great effort to prevent his mother from finding out. This kind of secretiveness became almost second nature to him, a habit which he made no effort to break. His mother's influence was strong enough to prevent Nock from renouncing his Holy Orders until her death in 1924, fourteen years after he ceased his active church activity.[10]

Eccentric or not, Nock was an editor equal to the best the country had produced. Lewis Mumford has touched on this ability recently.

He was the very model of the old-fashioned gentleman, American style: quiet spoken, fond of good food, punctilious in little matters of courtesy, with a fund of good stories, many of them western; never speaking about himself, never revealing anything directly about himself. . . . From time to time he gave me excellent advice, for which I am still grateful: as when I was trying to choose between two or three openings that I had found, he urged me first to ask myself what I *wanted* to do, before I made any judgment about feasibility or financial return. . . . He was at his best as a writer, however, in his unsigned contributions to the *Freeman*; for he wrote an easy, unstarched, colloquial prose, incomparably better than anything being written by his colleagues on the *New Republic* or

the *Nation*—or anywhere else. . . . [I] never lost my sense of gratitude for what I had learned from him, in the writing of prose, and
in the value of understatement.[11]

As Brooks wrote, "Perverse as he might have been, Nock was
somehow tonic, and his repose and distinction of style pervaded,
from end to end, a paper that was generally known as the best
written in the country." His notions of individuality forbade
any Mencken-like attempt to form writing styles after his own.
Nock cherished differences of style and opinion all his life, and
wished no imitators. The only standards he set up were those of
quality, both in subject and expression. Anyone with something
to say and ability to say it well could gain entrance to the *Freeman*'s columns.

Francis Neilson, the co-editor, touchy and overbearing and to
his death jealous of his partner's ability to write, took refuge in
charges of piracy. Nock, he charged, stole his ideas; the fact that
Neilson's ideas expressed in Neilson's ponderous prose were virtually unreadable he did not consider, and perhaps he did not
even know it. But many who knew Nock well cherished his memory. Perhaps Nock's secretary, friend, and confidante Suzanne
La Follette has best captured Nock's effect on those working for
him in a short memoir of the period. This exchange took place as
the *Freeman* was closing.

Nock's friend, Edward Epstean, told him, "You've done a great
deal for all those young people."

"I don't know that I've ever done anything for them except
leave them alone," Nock said.

"Yes, I understand," answered Epstean. "But if someone else
had been letting them alone, it would have been a very different
story."[12]

Nock seems to have been a hard man to sum up.

VI

When the *Freeman* was closing, three Philadelphians, Rebecca
Windsor and her sister and brother-in-law, Mr. and Mrs. Ed-

mund C. Evans, came to Nock in a final effort to keep the magazine going. When Nock explained that this was not in his power, they asked him if there were projects he had in mind personally. There were. He wished first to write a life of Jefferson, and then one of Rabelais. Nock enjoyed financial assistance from Mr. Evans, and after his death from the two women, at odd intervals throughout his life. Their help allowed him to do just exactly as he wished.

Jefferson, finished in 1926, was a small but long-lasting success, and still retains many admirers. The book on Rabelais, issued as both a separate essay and as an introduction to the complete text, is now dated by the subsequent work of the Rabelais Society, but remains an excellent introduction to the man's work.

While working on the biographies of Jefferson and Rabelais, Nock continued his output of essays as in the *Freeman* years. Most major magazines soon featured his work, and he enhanced his reputation both as theorist and prose stylist. In 1930, Suzanne La Follette, with the backing of Dr. Peter Fireman, began a new *Freeman* in an attempt to revive the standards of the old. Unfortunately, the depression dried up the subsidy, and the magazine failed after fifteen months. At the same time, Nock taught briefly at Bard under his close friend, Canon Bernard Iddings Bell, warden of the college and formerly president of St. Stephen's. While there, Nock delivered the 1931 Page–Barbour lectures at the University of Virginia. His ringing defense of the classical curriculum sounded to many like a voice from a musty museum, and only in retrospect is it possible to see that his work was one of the major salvos in the growing battle of educationists over the success of Dewey and his theories. In subsequent years, Nock published regularly: essays, a diary, a book of political theory, another biography, and so on.

But the world had changed suddenly, and with little change in basic ideas Nock found himself a conservative rather than a liberal or radical. Shocked at first, he finally assumed the name gladly, if only on his own terms. His essays soon placed him in the intellectual leadership of the conservative opposition to Roosevelt. In addition to the qualities of his mind and style, he had so little money that almost no one could accuse him of being a malefactor of great wealth. As usual, his thoughts were disinterested, in contrast to many of those who were so vocal during the period.

In 1936, Nock began a series of essays for the *American Mercury*, then under the leadership of fellow Players Club member Paul Palmer. This work, collectively entitled "The State of the Union," earned Nock the reputation that still colors much contemporary opinion of him. Palmer, like others before him, has described Nock's secretiveness and austerity, about which others had remarked in the *Freeman* years. Palmer respected Nock enormously, and evidently learned a great deal from the older man.

Nock was an editor's dream. "I suppose Nock was the greatest stylist among American writers," Palmer has written. "At least, no American ever wrote a purer prose. His command of simple words is the despair of his disciples." He was always courteous, punctual, and willing to take any constructive criticism. "His copy, when it came to me, was spotless, immaculate. . . . There were no vulgarisms, nothing slipshod, no clichés." This style did not come to Nock without effort. He rarely turned out more than three hundred words a day, always working and reworking with care. Almost all the corrections evident on surviving manuscripts were reductions in the number of words, exchanges of common words for uncommon, and minute changes to improve meter.

Palmer's recollection is indicative of the effect Nock could have on men who knew him well. Nock was a constant correspondent of Palmer, and a frequent visitor to his house. Palmer mentions the formidable mien which his friend had, and the attention to formality which existed between them for several years. First names did not come easily to Albert Nock, even with friends, and he could be acidly proper if anyone took such a liberty with him. Palmer was put in his place once for such a *gaffe*, and only after close editorial and personal contact did the great day come: ". . . at last, one notable day, I received a letter commencing, 'Dear Paul.' It was the accolade: I felt that then I

might be ready for the company of the great, even if only at the
foot of the table. The first time I called him 'Albert' to his face
was somehow like my first cigar, my graduation from boot camp
in the Marine Corps, my first hour at a desk marked EDITOR;
I was a man." That which was hard to possess—familiarity with
Nock—had a special value. Nock's manner could offend some,
but those who endured it felt amply rewarded. Nock may have
been impossible to know, but he was easy to respect.[13]

VII

The war years did not treat Nock kindly. America is not particularly pleasant toward those who oppose her ventures in uniform; she accuses dissenters of all sorts of crimes. During World
War II, the opprobrious names were "Nazi," "anti-Semite," and
so on. Such terms were also extended to Nock's friends; Frank
Chodorov, a man devoted to Nock and his ideals, found himself
enduring the label "anti-Semitic Jew" for his opposition to American intervention in the war. As usual, when confronted by that
of which he disapproved, Nock ignored it. The world went to
war without Albert Nock. Fortunately, *Harper's* editor, William
Briggs, kept after him to do his autobiography. Nock, living in
virtual seclusion on Canaan Mountain and seeing only Miss Wilson, except for his occasional visits with Ruth Robinson, H. L.
Mencken, and Palmer, worked steadily for two years. His book,
The Memoirs of a Superfluous Man, was quite successful, far
beyond his hopes. Indeed, so many people bought it, Nock began to think it was of little worth. Or so he said.

Nock's health gradually deteriorated. His eyes bothered him,
and he had trouble remembering dates and directions. Nevertheless, he began editing a small sheet of book reviews for the
National Economic Council. Soon, the disease was too much for
him and he took to bed at Miss Robinson's. The "quacks," as he
called them, diagnosed lymphatic leukemia. He died on August
19, 1945. Miss Robinson, well-instructed, notified Canon Bell, a
frequent visitor to her home. He conducted a simple Episcopal

service in her studio. Nock was buried in the Riverside Cemetery at Wakefield, Rhode Island, in the South County he loved.

Frank Chodorov remembered Nock as "the most civilized man I ever knew. He was knowledgeable but never pedantic, reserved but companionable, cosmopolitan in his tastes and, above all, a gentleman to whom it never occurred to inflict hurt on any man."[14] Ellery Sedgwick, the old *Atlantic* editor, put into words what most of Nock's friends must have felt about the man. "After all," he wrote, "the last refuge of individuality is the rock of prejudice. On that rock Albert Nock was founded. Prejudices, immovable, ineradicable, Gargantuan, buttressed him on every side. They made him one of the persons of his type. A more inviolate and inviolable personality I have never known. I love and respect his memory. Something unique has gone out of the world."[15]

Something unique had indeed gone out of the world, for besides having a unique personality, Nock had unknowingly played a unique role in movements that did not flower until years after his death. Some of his ideas, especially in education, had influence while he was alive, and continue to influence. Robert Maynard Hutchins, Mortimer Adler, and Stringfellow Barr carried the notion of classical education into the Great Books program. Writers like Mark Van Doren, Mortimer Smith, and Arthur Bestor spelled out in detail the values which the useless knowledge of the liberal experience gives a student. Jacques Barzun, perhaps the most influential and erudite of all, emphasized the small number of people capable of enjoying the good things of life, and warned of the evils of trying to educate those who could only be trained. The degree of influence Nock may have had on these men is not measurable. One can detect a definite influence on Barzun, and lesser traces in Van Doren and Smith. No one can say for sure. But the movement toward what Arthur Bestor calls the restoration of learning, begun by Nock, Flexner, and others, was responsible for much of the new educational emphasis on formative learning. John Dewey's system, undisputed in 1920, was in the 1950's in retreat before Russian scientific superiority and the wide dissatisfaction on the part of parents with the products of the public schools.

Nock's influence also can be found in present-day organizations. His friend Frank Chodorov, working on Nock's idea that education must always precede action, was instrumental in founding *Analysis*, then another *Freeman*, with John Chamberlain, Henry Hazlitt, and Suzanne La Follette, and the Intercollegiate Society of Individualists. Leonard Read, whom Nock knew late in life, helped establish the Foundation for Economic Education, dedicated to the spread of knowledge on free enterprise and Jeffersonian political principles. A group of clergymen, calling themselves the Remnant, meets regularly to discuss the theological aspects of capitalistic free society. One of its leaders, the Reverend Mr. Edmund Opitz, has been greatly influenced by Nock's work. And so it goes. Perhaps these organizations would flourish now even if Nock had never lived. But he did live, and many of these men read him, talked to him, and agreed with him. His influence is intangible, hard to measure; but it seems to exist nevertheless.

But the unique thing which went out of the world with Nock was a phenomenon of synthesis. Nock, for all his vagaries, despite the outwardly miscellaneous nature of his roots, was a key figure in the development of what is today the intellectual right wing in American political thought. The terms "radical" and "conservative," he pointed out in his discussion of Lucius Cary, were not of necessity mutually exclusive. The same might be said today. In the context of American history, much of the radical right is a Jeffersonian movement, in opposition to the Hamiltonian path of liberalism. Its emphasis on decentralization, on self-reliance, on noninvolvement in the affairs of other nations, on low tariffs, and its rural as opposed to urban support—all these are Jeffersonian in derivation and emphasis. Yet, because of the nature of the two-party system in America, the issue has been obscured because the traditional Tories also have a place on the right. The Tory wants government to help business, to erect tariffs, to use American power in the affairs of other countries; on occasion, he even wishes to support public morality by state action in such fields as censorship or public religion. These things are very far from the ideals of Jefferson. The Tory and Jeffersonian now oppose the Hamiltonian liberals, but their alliance is an uneasy one.

Nock, in his writings and his character, provided a possible synthesis of the two strains of modern rightist thought. If, he might have said, one combines the means of Spencer with the ends of Arnold to produce a tradition a Burke can revere; if, that is, one could make the basically radical ethic of Jefferson a tradition—then one would have the ideal basis for a radical conservatism. Nock's radical impulses tempered by his conservative mind showed how this could be accomplished by a man. America showed how this could happen in a country. In his inviolable personality, serene on his rock of prejudice, Nock has proved to be the godfather of a new Jeffersonian child in America. Many aspects of the movement he would disapprove of. Indeed, the idea of a society of individualists, of conservatives proclaiming their distaste for the status quo, might well bring a twinkle into his eyes. But at least the movement exists, contradictory or not. Having stood, perplexed, aside from so much sorrow, he pointed the way for others, who might be able to profit from his work.

CHAPTER TWO

A TRADITION

O NE of the most persistent debates in America centers around the true meaning of the word "liberal." To many, the word carries good connotations, not of specific good things, perhaps, but rather a suggestion of that with which the historian likes to be identified. "Liberal" connotes reform, freedom, political action, a state of mind favorable to intellectual improvement, and a number of other images which are attractive. Only when one attempts to define the word precisely does the trouble begin. Senator Taft and Franklin Roosevelt both considered themselves liberals; John Steinbeck and John Dos Passos both wrote novels that were considered liberal. Yet there were great differences in the philosophies of all these men. How, then, can all somehow qualify for the label "liberal"?

In a recent book,[1] Charles Forcey discusses what he calls the "crossroads of liberalism"—the time, just before World War I, when the liberal movement, then a reasonably coherent whole, had to choose between two conflicting and mutually exclusive paths. Liberals could adopt the leadership and ideals of Theodore Roosevelt and attempt to achieve social justice through a centralized federal government, a watchful tolerance of the trusts, and what Herbert Croly called a "New Nationalism"—an attempt to realize the American dream through use of Hamiltonian means. They could also choose to reject those means and attempt to follow the tradition of Thomas Jefferson, placing emphasis on the small businessman, the "Forgotten Man" of William Graham Sumner, and the virtues of the Protestant Ethic—

thrift, personal religion, and self-reliance. Forcey, in his study, traces the path of the Hamiltonians, which he believes to be the true liberal path. I will attempt to follow the path of a man who remained true to his own interpretation of Thomas Jefferson.

The important distinction between the Hamiltonian and the Jeffersonian liberals is one of method. Both groups may be considered "liberal" or even "radical," in the sense that the members of each felt little personal or ideological identification with men who were satisfied with existing conditions. Both groups believed in equality of opportunity and the need for reform. But where one group, the Hamiltonians, sought this end through concentration of power and the use of federal force, the other shrank from large government in any form, and called for localism of the sort Jefferson advocated.

Here is the core of the difficulty of definition. Those who retained the desire for equalitarian ends, while considering the old means unequal to the task, felt that they deserved to inherit the name "liberal." Those who felt that they retained both the ends and the means thought that their claims to the term were even more valid. The dispute continues.

The paths of these two groups split in 1912, the Hamiltonians following Roosevelt and the New Nationalism, the Jeffersonians following Wilson and the New Freedom. But shortly, dismayed by the jingoism of their hero, Roosevelt's supporters slowly left him to join the Jeffersonians in voting for Wilson in 1916. This exodus ended when Wilson announced his policy of intervention. Those who had supported Roosevelt favored fighting. Those who had originally supported Wilson remained pacifists, and were often severely harassed by their former leader, who also, incidentally, vastly increased the domain of the government he was supposed to minimize. During the twenties, both groups wrote mainly for the smaller magazines—the *New Masses*, the *Dial*, the *Freeman*, the *New Republic*, and on occasion, even H. L. Mencken's "high tory" *American Mercury*. But the difference in method remained as deep as ever and only appeared less so in the common hostility to the businessmen in the White

House. Many of the men were close friends during this period despite their differences, and in many cases worked on the same magazines.

Although their common dislike appeared to unite these men, their differences were in fact never resolved, even in the twenties. The nature of the split, however, only became obvious to the public with the advent of the New Deal. Both groups had supported Franklin Roosevelt because of their distaste for Hoover, but when Roosevelt began to expand the welfare roles, the bureaucracy, and the national debt—generally staking his position along the Hamiltonian lines of big, centralized government—the Jeffersonians revolted. When they did so, they found to their shock that they were aligned with the very forces of inertia, philistinism, and business that they had so detested in the twenties. Common hatreds gave these old-line liberals the same political position as the old-line Tories, and thus the old liberals and the Tories became identified in the common mind. Most of the single taxers, most of the pacifists, the anarchists, and a number of other intellectuals followed this path. Charles A. Beard wrote the history, H. L. Mencken the diatribes. John Dos Passos wrote the novels, and Ralph Adams Cram spoke for the artists. Others who switched their allegiance from left to right would include John Chamberlain, William Henry Chamberlin, and Max Eastman. Many of these men disliked their new Tory allies fully as much as did Mr. Roosevelt.

The New Deal, however, also posed a problem for the historian of tradition. Despite its Hamiltonian trappings and the Hamiltonian predilections of New Deal godfathers, such as Croly and Lippmann, the men who supported much of the New Deal felt called upon to clothe their plans in Jeffersonian trappings. Never, indeed, was a man called upon by so many to prove so much. Conservatives like Nicholas Murray Butler and James Truslow Adams made Jefferson a conservative, in favor of restricted government powers, individual liberty, a less nationalistic trade policy, and so on. Southern agrarians supported the landed aristocracy as the bulwark of an individualistic, rural, nonmaterialistic way of life which they felt best expressed Jefferson's desires. On the left, Henry Wallace termed the New Deal "a twentieth century model of Jefferson's principles of government." John Dewey found the pragmatic spirit of the movement the very essence of Jeffersonianism: had not the great man entrusted the government to the people of the living generation? T. V. Smith thought that democracy was "not a goal," but "a going. Democracy is whatever can be arrived at democratically." Charles Wiltse found true Jeffersonianism not in specific policies, but in a spirit. He thought Jefferson's true legacy was "not his solution to the political problem, but his realization that the problem must be solved anew in each succeeding era."[2]

Discussion of the right and wrong of these various strands will achieve little. What must be realized is that every man had his own Jefferson, and that these men fell into general groups. Nock fell into the first group, and for the purposes of clarity this body of men will be called the "Jeffersonian group" throughout this book. The New Dealers, because of their Hamiltonian heritage from the era of the first Roosevelt and their affection for the Hamiltonian method, will remain Hamiltonians, with no particular judgment applied to the reasonableness of their claim as true descendents of the third president. In its major forms— omitting the agrarians and more bizarre manifestations of Jeffersonianism, like the work of Ezra Pound—the Jeffersonian tradition is a dual tradition, one branch a method, the other a spirit, and there the matter will have to rest.

Within the Jeffersonian group, then, Nock moved as a figure of importance. He was a Jeffersonian in 1912, during the Wilson campaign, and he remained one during the war, when Wilson did not. He continued unchanged in the twenties, opposing the smug materialism of the Coolidge era. He remained, after an era of Franklin Roosevelt, still loyal to the cause. Nock is of historical importance in one sense because his thought is a key to this group and its development. In a time obsessed with material rewards, his ideas on manners and the proper field for the exercise of personal choice found a small but loyal audience. His essays on education also merited permanence for their role in the movement to restore learning and scholarship to schools that had degenerated into "adjustment centers" under educators calling themselves disciples of John Dewey. Finally, as a stylist of the American language, Nock produced two works that will live as American classics, his biography of Jefferson and his memoirs, and he developed the essay as an art form to the point where his editors despaired of finding his equal.

In a sense, Nock was an atypical member of the group of Jeffersonian liberals. He did not share their rather naïve faith in the abilities of men to improve and rule themselves. Toward the end of his life, he turned to formulating a social philosophy which bore only faint resemblance to the optimism and faith in mankind which characterized his earlier years. In many ways, his was a philosophy of frustration, for like many of his colleagues he had been a believer in human goodness, rationality, and improvability. In his later books, however, he brought his theories into line with his observations of men in action. Nock's philosophy was not a cheerful one. It assumed that most men were incapable of living in real freedom, but that there were a few who must have a great deal of freedom in order to grow. Only the latter were capable of producing the minds and wills which could improve the lot of the former; Nock devoted his life to the nourishment of this remnant.

II

The Jeffersonian tradition got its name, if not its policies, from the man who came to symbolize democracy. As Jefferson himself constantly reiterated, his formulations were not original; they were "in the air," and he merely verbalized them. What, then, does the Jeffersonian tradition include?

Jefferson, through his policies, intended to make it possible for every citizen to enjoy the good life. The good life can mean many things to many people. To Jefferson, it meant education for the gifted, an economic system that had a place for all who would work, land for men to live on and own, and a government that would leave men alone and not force allegiance to religious, monarchical, or economic demands. The one word for these ideal conditions is "civilization."

This belief in civilization, in an atmosphere of freedom which would enable everyone to pursue and develop his own desires, had numerous implications. The doctrine of equal opportunity was paramount. The path to knowledge and civilization lay in education, freedom, and independence. The Jeffersonian system of education was élitist: all were to be given an elementary education. The "boy of best genius" in each school would then attend grammar school (girls were excluded). These survivors would continue a year or two, and then all but the best would be dropped. These best, if they could keep up the work, would eventually reach college—would be "raked from the rubbish annually." Thus no talented man, solely because of poverty, would be deprived of the benefits of a liberal education.[3]

For opportunity to flourish, there must be rightful liberty: "Of liberty then I would say," Jefferson wrote in 1819, "that, in the whole plenitude of its extent, it is unobstructed action according to our will, but rightful liberty is unobstructed action according to our will within limits drawn around us by the equal rights of others."[4] The definition was stated in terms of action, but it was felt in terms of the mind: "I have sworn on the altar of God eternal hostility to every form of tyranny over the mind of man."[5] This belief caused him to think so highly of Virginia's statute of religious freedom that he wished to be remembered only as the father of it, of the University of Virginia, and of the Declaration of Independence.

The right to grow by oneself, to develop one's own character regardless of the pressures of others, led to two further doctrines: individualism and the hatred of politics. Above all, one must be true to oneself: "I never submitted the whole system of my opinions to the creed of any party of men whatever," he wrote pointedly, "in religion, in philosophy, in politics, or in anything else where I was capable of thinking for myself." Anyone who did this had achieved "the last degradation of a free and moral agent. If I could not go to heaven but with a party, I would not go there at all."[6]

From this opinion developed the suspicion of politics. The political man, to a degree far greater than any other, must be responsive to the wills of others. Indeed, if he is to win votes, he must be an ideological weathervane, pointing in the direction of the strongest wind. At least, this was the case with many politicians, and was a pressure on all. Further, Jefferson felt that spoils, and not statesmanship, were the goals of most office seekers; and with this in mind he wrote that "whenever a man has cast a longing eye on offices, a rottenness begins in his conduct."[7] Such a man could no longer be true to himself; he was trying to go to heaven with a party.

The attainment of liberty, and its care and feeding, was a delicate matter which especially concerned Jefferson. His great fears were of unchecked power, centralization, and size—all of which overlap: "What has destroyed liberty and the rights of man in every government which has ever existed under the sun?" he asked. "The generalizing and concentrating all cares and powers into one body, no matter whether of the autocrats of Russia or France, or of the aristocrats of a Venetian senate."[8] The central government must be limited internally, leaving most affairs to the states and communities; its main function is to present a united front in foreign affairs. Its object is simply to enable the people to retain control over their representatives. "The article . . . nearest my heart is the division of the country into wards,"[9] he wrote, because history has shown that rights and liberty flourish in inverse proportion to the amount of centralization.

Americans had particular reason to be wary of governmental power. Many, if not most of them, had left Europe to escape autocracies, corruption, religious persecution, or war service. They therefore wished no part of European affairs, and ardently hoped that government in any form would simply leave them alone.[10] With this feeling came a pacifism that caused men to regard all war as imperialist venturing with which true democrats should have nothing to do.

The final major article of faith in the Jeffersonian tradition was the almost mystic attitude taken toward the soil and the agrarian life. The cities, like European life as a whole, were corrupting, immoral, unclean; the farm was good. "Those who labor in the earth are the chosen people of God, if ever He had a chosen people, whose breasts He had made His peculiar deposit of substantial and genuine virtue," he wrote in the *Notes on Virginia*. "It is the focus in which He keeps alive that sacred fire, which otherwise might escape from the face of the earth." Nowhere in history had there ever been found an example of mass moral corruption among the tillers of the soil. Immorality "is the mark set upon those, who, not looking up to heaven, to their own soil and industry, as does the husbandman, for their subsistence, depend for it on the casualties and caprice of customers."[11]

The minor tenets of Jeffersonian thought tended to be less important and less consistently held. They were generally used by those who called on them as supporting arguments rather than main ones. They were persistent, however, and were held by a great many people who considered themselves Jeffersonians. They were occasionally chosen to carry main burdens—especially in political campaigns where appeals to prejudice might garner votes. They included a basic antipathy to England, for her powers over the American economy and her generally bad manners; an antipathy to the "interests," i.e., any group either big or wealthy, and thus corrupted by money and distance from the soil; a belief in strong minority rights in a system where government was purely negative; free trade; and the idea of a natural aristocracy, explicitly stated by Jefferson[12] and yet often submerged or forgotten by his followers.

The overriding purpose of Jeffersonian politics, then, was to achieve an environment in which men could pursue the good life as they saw fit. The necessary conditions for this environment, and their corollaries, may be summed up as follows: equal opportunity for all; as much freedom from restraint as was consistent with the maintenance of order and the freedom of others; education for all who could profit by it, without regard for economic circumstances; the furthering of the morally superior rural life over the urban; the need for each man to be true to himself, and, if necessary, to ignore the opinions of others; dislike of politics; local government, subjected to severe checks and balances to prevent anyone from gaining unnecessary power over others; avoidance of foreign entanglements, including war and diplomacy, as undesirable for democratic America; and minor tenets: Anglophobia, free trade, antimonopoly feeling, and élitism.

These were the elements in and the necessary conditions of the tradition. Its course, for the fifty years between the death of Jefferson and the rise of Henry George, is not the subject of this book.[13] This tradition supplied the vocabulary for the Jacksonian era. It motivated the Whigs to abandon the trappings of conservatism and parade William Henry Harrison around like a chip from the old log cabin. It prepared the public mind to see in Lincoln the embodiment of the qualities Americans believed to be American. The important thing is that the tradition existed, that it was believed and widely held, and that it supplied the language many men used when they expressed their views. An understanding of these attitudes is the first great step toward placing Henry George, the muckrakers, the progressives, and much of the opposition to the New Deal in the nineteen thirties in proper historical perspective. Albert Jay Nock adopted a virtually pure version of the Jeffersonian philosophy as his own when he entered public life. The course and development of his faith is the subject of this study.

How did Nock understand and interpret the Jeffersonian ideals? First, he attempted to show the people, through magazine articles, where improvements could be made in American life. Then, he attempted to achieve the Jeffersonian ideal of civilized life in the editorship of a literary magazine of the highest quality. Third, he analyzed the American educational system and outlined a means of remedying defects which he found there. Fourth, he turned his attention to morals and manners, in an attempt to realize a society more hospitable to the enjoyment of the good life. Finally, he attempted an analysis of the state to show where this institution helped, and where it threatened, the enjoyment of the good life.

During these years, Nock was speaking not only for himself, but for many of his fellow liberals, radicals, and conservatives, as well as groups of largely inarticulate people. His beliefs had their basis in American history. In his attempt to formulate and organize his beliefs, he has a story to tell everyone who is interested in the intellectual and political development of the United States.

CHAPTER THREE

THE JEFFERSONIAN AS A LIBERAL:

The *American Magazine*, 1910–14

DATING the start of the progressive movement is difficult. As early as 1871, Henry George published *Our Land and Land Policy*, a document which, if not always included in the progressive movement by historians, nevertheless deserves mention. A strong admirer of Jefferson, George attacked the status quo on the issue of land monopoly. Like Jefferson, he was a proponent of localism, free trade, minimum government, maximum liberty, and the good life. His vision of early American utopia was full of the agrarian virtues and simple pleasures which Jefferson lauded. The dream, although often intended for cities, was primarily pastoral. "There are gratifications," George wrote, "for the social and intellectual nature—for that part of the man that rises above the animal. The power of sympathy, the sense of companionship, the emulation of comparison and contrast, open a wider, and fuller, and more varied life. In rejoicing, there are others to rejoice; in sorrow the mourners do not mourn alone. There are husking bees, and apple parings, and quilting parties. . . ."[1] The *Volk*, in agrarian purity, could regain this utopia via the tax on land rent.

In 1897, George's death removed one of Jefferson's greatest champions. Almost simultaneously came the birth of a new movement within progressive ranks. While George was making his last campaign for the mayoralty of New York, under the party label of "The Democracy of Thomas Jefferson," S. S. Mc-

Clure, one of the magnates of the magazine industry, began a campaign to educate and reassure Americans about one of their greatest worries: the trust. The campaign was at first haphazard, even coincidental. As McClure told the story, at the time of the Chicago World's Fair, he had sent a representative to the Armour Institute of Technology to do a story on the Institute, its head, Dr. Frank W. Gunsaulus, and its namesake, Mr. Philip D. Armour. This story started McClure thinking about possible articles on the achievements of American businesses, specifically Standard Oil. The project expanded the more it was discussed. By February, 1897, talk about trusts had become general, and the outlook for a successful series seemed good. McClure felt that most people feared the trusts out of ignorance, and that the best way to inform them was "not by taking the matter up abstractly, but to take one Trust, and to give its history, its effects, and its tendencies."[2] Because Ida Tarbell had lived in the oil region of Pennsylvania and had watched Standard Oil develop and put her father out of business, she was put to work on the series. Not until five years later did she finish what became one of the most influential books of the era.

Meanwhile, Lincoln Steffens, a newly hired *McClure's* staff man, was given a roving commission to familiarize himself with the ways in which magazine staff writers did their work. Once embarked on a tour of corrupt midwestern cities, Steffens discovered St. Louis, and became so interested in conditions there that he wrote the first of the so-called "muckraking" articles. It reached print shortly before the first installment of Miss Tarbell's Standard Oil story.

Even then, the issue of Hamilton vs. Jefferson was being considered. Could people be trusted, or must they be coerced for their own good? Steffens himself was in doubt, although he leaned toward the Hamiltonian means. At one time he wrote that Hamilton "understood and formulated his political theories and policies on the principle of a government by a privileged, superior class. He distrusted the people and he was right in this; the American people have in the long run followed him and not

Jefferson, who trusted them. And wasn't Hamilton fundamentally right?" But later he reconsidered, and expressed no preference: "Hamilton and Jefferson again, and it remains to be seen which is the better way."[3]

For McClure and Miss Tarbell, however, Jefferson was the predominating impulse. Miss Tarbell was firmly in the camp of the agrarians by temperament, even though she spent most of her time analyzing industrial and urban problems. "I believe," she wrote, "that the connection of men and women with the soil is not only most healthy for the body but essential for the mind and the soul. . . ."[4] McClure, in his belief in the local, commission form of government that he had seen working in Europe, echoed the Jeffersonian sentiments of his colleagues; all preferred local, decentralized democracy. Like most Jeffersonian solutions, a commission form of government was a practical, simple, and local cure for a specific evil, and depended to a great degree on the ability of the people for self-cure, once their ills had been shown them. As Alfred Kazin has summed up the predilections of most progressive journalists: "The muckraker's apotheosis was always the same—a vision of small, quiet lives humbly and usefully led; a transcription of Jeffersonian small-village ideals for a generation bound to megalopolis, yet persistently nostalgic for the old-fashioned peace and the old-fashioned ideal."[5]

McClure's chief lieutenant was John S. Phillips, a deeply intellectual man who, William Allen White reports, had "a spark of genius" and knew it. He and McClure did not get along, and eventually, in 1905, Phillips and a group of *McClure's* writers put out feelers for and eventually bought *Leslie's Monthly*. They renamed their acquisition *The American Magazine*, and "started out to carry the torch of an evolutionary revolution to the world." Around him, Phillips gathered the best of the progressive writers: Ray Stannard Baker, Finley Peter Dunne, John Siddall, Miss Tarbell, Steffens, and White. The magazine, White wrote later, "was an organ of propaganda wrapped in the tinfoil of a literary quality which at least reflected the temper of the times."

The goals of the magazine differed with each individual. To Steffens it was "a feast of fun" which enabled him to free-lance with little attention to any greater purpose. To William Allen White, it was part of a great movement, "a world movement, [in which we were] doing and thinking what men all over Christendom were doing and thinking; we were trying to establish all over the civilized world more equitable human relations."[6] To Miss Tarbell, the idea of enlightenment and education was paramount: "*The American Magazine* had little genuine muckraking spirit. It did have a large and fighting interest in fair play; it sought to present things as they were, not as somebody thought they ought to be. We were journalists, not propagandists; and as journalists we sought new angles on old subjects."[7] It was, in other words, the duty of the writers for the magazine to rake up the good with the bad, the success with the failure. It was their task to show what had worked in the past to those who needed help in the present. It was an attempt to improve and educate, not to shock or irritate. All staff members would have echoed Ray Stannard Baker, when he wrote many years later, "Truth is always sensational, cutting like a keen fresh wind through the fog of pretense and secrecy, and the slime of corruption."[8]

II

Into this atmosphere of accuracy, high purpose, and talent came Albert Jay Nock late in 1909. To Steffens, he was "that finished scholar, [who] put in mastered English for us editorials which expressed with his grave smile and chuckling tolerance 'our' interpretations of things human."[9] Although he never wrote about it publicly, Nock moved into public life as a journalist because of a certain feeling of uselessness and insularity in his parish duties. Apparently, also, his call had come as much from his domineering mother as from a higher source, and after ten years he had had enough. "My life was detached, untouched and colourless,"[10] he later wrote to a close friend about those years, and that was the extent of his comment on his ministerial career.

Four years of the classics, philosophy, and mathematics had trained Nock's mind well. His policy, like that of his fellow writers, was to prod, encourage, and point the way for reform-minded people who were capable of exercising leadership. In one offhand remark in a later article, he illustrated the manner in which many of the progressives thought. "It is not important to dwell on this or that remedy, for as soon as a social disorder is really understood it is already more than half cured. Diagnosis is the important thing. . . ."[11] "Diagnosis" here means a demonstration of fact, of existing conditions—another way of expressing "education." Both terms imply the Jeffersonian concept that all people, regardless of their station, can be improved by education and the leadership of those whom they choose. All that people need is to know the truth.

Implied, too, in these articles, especially in the numerous ones on taxation, is the Jeffersonian idea that all men should have the opportunity to rise economically and intellectually. Nock, by writing, was trying to translate economic realities into terms readily understandable by everybody. By so doing, he was improving the climate for change: "If the plain people of this country could once be brought to feel—not to sense in a vague, inattentive way, for a passing moment, but really to *feel*—the incubus of their indirect taxation, they would overhaul our institutions with as merciless a hand, I fear, as the plain people of France, under similar provocation, once laid upon theirs."[12] Because economic democracy was the necessary prerequisite for political democracy, *The American Magazine* writers concentrated on the injustices of discriminatory taxation, corruption, speculation, or monopoly. They did not, however, lose sight of the Jeffersonian objective which all of them seem to have retained somewhere in the back of their minds. Often the goal was bypassed or forgotten, but always it reappeared, in sometimes mystic terms, as the utopian goal of the progressive intellectuals: the attainment of the benefits of civilization—in jobs, education, freedom—for all men. The magazine, Nock wrote, was primarily interested in civilization, "The humane life lived to the highest power by as many persons as possible." Civilization presupposed "a fair and decent economic environment; and taxation is the very taproot of economics. That is why we are interested in taxation. We are interested in promoting sound and practicable tax-reforms only because we want to help create economic circumstances that will take off all immoral pressure from every man, and enable him to be just as good as he might be and as he really wants to be, and would be if he had the power."[13]

To a degree quite beyond that of most magazines of large circulation, the editors of *The American Magazine* were themselves practitioners of the good life as they understood it. Indicative of the combined humor, erudition, art, and occasional chaos of life at the *American* was a poem that staff member John Reed, later a famous Communist, printed privately while he was still a writer for the magazine. Most of the poem concerned a day in the life of a Greenwich Village resident. The part on the magazine went, in part:

NOCK, clasping Matthew Arnold to his heart,—
An anarchist in everything but Art!
AGRICOLA MINERVA TARBELL:—I,
Rejected verse in hand, and fire in mine eye!
"What's up?" says SIDDALL, nervous, "Poetry?
"My God! This is no place for low-brow me!"
MONACHUS opens: "Verse is our disgrace!
"Where in these days is the true singer's place?
"Sure *ars poetica* is on the wane,—
"The last month's magazine gives me a pain!"
"It's my best choice," says PHILLIPS, "What is yours?"
"See *Century, Atlantic* or *McClure's!*"
"Ridiculous!"—"The poets all abhor us!"—
"Our verse is rotten!" NOCK and I in chorus;
"REED'S going to cast another pearl before us!"—
"I am!" I answer with an angry hiss,
Tapping my poem, "What is wrong with this?"
"THE MINSTREL OF ROMANCE"—"No Harmony—"
Cries Nock, "To much *cacoethes scribendi*—

"Genus irritabile vatum—" "You should read
"Your Matthew Arnold—" "Arnold! Huh! Indeed!
"A polished strengthless sapless hide-bound bard—"
"Walt Whitman? Hardware cataloguing by the yard—"
"Foot—rhythm—rhyme—stanza—Sapphics—Lessing—Pope—
"Hellenic—Dionysius—couplet—trope—"
"Horace—" ("Assistance!" cries the SID, "Police!")
"Poetic laws—" (NOCK) "Hold!" says PHILLIPS, "Peace!"
"Down with the stilted numbers of the Schools
"For rules were made for Art not Art for Rules!
"Poetry is—at least I hold it so—
"Poetry's—" (Gesture), (Gesture), "—er—you know—"
Nock's theory, in short, is full of holes—
"Sir Hudson Maxim or the Reverend Bowles!"
MONACHUS bludgeons us with ancient Greek,
French, Latin, Hebrew—and I take a sneak,
Most cannily escaping from the battle
Now raging o'er a phrase of Aristotle![14]

In such an erudite atmosphere, no dead hand of dogma retarded the operations of the journalists. They were doctrinaire only in that they wished always to write the truth, regardless of who was helped or hurt by their disclosures. Some may have preferred socialism over the existing system. Others believed in a sharply regulated nation of small businesses. Nock, philosophically, felt that Henry George, in *Progress and Poverty* and other books, had laid the best groundwork for a reasonably equalitarian state within the Jeffersonian tradition. He did not, however, let his affinity for the single tax blind him in his recommendations. He was, he wrote Leonard Read later, not an advocate of the single tax, he merely believed in it. Rarely, in any of the articles he wrote, was there a mention of the method of Henry George for obtaining social justice. Instead, Nock typically first pointed out the inequity in a current law, and second, showed how this specific evil could be remedied. In response to letters, he remarked that he did not wish to "escape the responsibility" of saying that he was "a single-taxer and, naturally, a free-trader." But this was a small matter. No matter how visionary he might be, he thought it unlikely that a magazine of large circulation would allow him to recommend reforms he knew were not immediately practicable. "The single-tax (as I think, unfortunately) is not one of these. The abolition of the general property tax, however, is a reform of far-reaching import and immediate practicability."[15]

The property tax occupied Nock's time almost totally for over a year. From December, 1910, through August, 1911, he appeared monthly in a series of articles entitled "The Things That Are Caesar's." The series opened with long, detailed analyses, with exhausting documentation, of what was wrong with the tax laws of various states. The basic demand was that, for the sake of the ignorant or impoverished small entrepreneur—as well as for common honesty—the tax on any property other than land should be eliminated. This property tax was referred to as "class legislation," because loopholes enabled a man of wealth totally to evade, if he so desired, any tax at all. Ability to pay was not taken into account, the thrifty were penalized, and, most tragic, most of the evasions were not even illegal. Taxes on movables were self-defeating, Nock argued, since the taxed would simply move their property when tax time came. A man with numerous residences would have his legal residence in a low or non-tax area, and thus technically he could not be taxed for his other estates because he was legally not a local citizen.

Once these inequities had been outlined, Nock pointed to Canada for the remedy. First, Canada had a responsible form of government, modeled after that of the British. There were no checks and balances, no impeding Supreme Court, and no constitutional prohibitions. Because of these conditions, informed popular will led by intelligent men had been able to institute tax reform, most notably in the far West. Speculation was controlled by a strict limit on the number of acres one person could buy, and by taxes that were higher on the unimproved land than on the improved land. But most important of all was the basic, necessary doctrine of the right of public property—a doctrine that had been lost in the United States. Canada's land policy, Nock wrote, enabled the Dominion government to hold all valuable public lands, including timber, mineral, and water rights, as public property not for sale. "There isn't enough money in all England or the United States," he quoted one Canadian official, "to buy a single acre. The reason is that the Dominion *wants citizens, not speculators.*" Canada had no land grants, either, and had a great distaste for "development by private enterprise" as practiced south of the border. "The moral influence of this policy is very striking," Nock continued. "I had a particular interest in observing its educational effect on the thousands of our people who are moving over into Canada each year. It has given them a clear idea of that fundamental doctrine of democracy, THE RIGHT OF PUBLIC PROPERTY."[16] Alberta taxed only land, not improvements, business, or incomes. She had tried them all, and returned to the land tax as the most just, the most equitable, and the easiest to administer.

What was attractive about Canada was the effect which her tax policies, as well as other advantages, had on her civilization. Democratic rule, contact with the older civilizations of the Commonwealth, the bilingual nature of the culture, and the tremendous commerce all helped to create a kind of Jeffersonian utopia in the north. But the most important aspect of Canadian life was that its civilization was "interesting. It is not without faults and those faults are not our faults. But all other considerations aside, Canadian civilization, especially as seen in its cities and towns, has a quality that ours has not—it has amenity, it is *amiable.* One loves it because it is lovely. It has an air of solvency, simplicity and depth of purpose that powerfully engages the human spirit by the side of sentiment and imagination."[17]

Nock's early articles on taxation, then, attempted to achieve the framework for a Jeffersonian civilization of amiable, educated people, who were not oppressed by the economic or social climate of their country. His views implied a certain faith in the capabilities of men for improvement, yet included a dislike of the impedimenta of the checks and balances of the American constitutional system. The people, Nock felt, had to be trusted to experiment with various plans, and thus by trial and error to discover that form of government and economic life which was best suited to them. These articles were only preludes to a large variety of writings.

Like other liberals in the pre-war years, Nock was a champion of experimentalism and a foe of systems. Those devices which seemed to have some possibility of leading to a better life, he was in favor of attempting, and he had few qualms about displacing hallowed orthodoxies. It was a time for such a position. In philosophy, John Dewey was attacking formal logic and the rigidity of the classical education. In history, Charles Beard was gathering material to show that economics and self-interest might have had more to do with the Constitution than faith in the spirit of democracy. In law, Justice Holmes was adapting history and experience to his profession, developing the school of legal realism and showing that more than mere logical deduction was necessary for justice. Intellectuals in many areas were interested in experiment, unafraid of new ideas, and, above all, looking for programs that worked, that produced tangible results, and that helped the majority.

Even the terminology betrayed the experimental atmosphere. Words like *new, adventure, expediency, responsibility to the public*, and so on signified the departure from the old norms of thought. Some of this enthusiasm was carried to amusing extremes: witness Nock's article in praise of Mr. Frank Gilbreth and his contributions to increased efficiency on the part of medical students while operating—on the face of a logical transfer of principle from one business to another, but somehow producing an effect that is not intended.[18] Nock also emphasized the man who succeeded because of a combination of Christian virtue and application of the rigors of the Protestant ethic. Everyone, regardless of background or environment, could succeed by diligence, hard work, and the proper humility, even in the America laid bare by the pens of the muckrakers.[19] In addition, Nock had no aversion to social activity on the part of the state: mothers' allowances, regulatory taxation, government ownership of the railroads, and so on were discussed calmly, even if not entirely recommended. One can sense, on the part of

Nock and his fellow writers, a definite willingness to try anything once, on a provisional basis, and yet a realization that pan-
aceas, while they make stirring reading and can win admiration,
generally cause more trouble than they cure.

A sense of a mythical America surrounded the "interesting
people" Nock described in the columns by that name. These
people, one sensed, were the repositories of the Jeffersonian
virtues, the descendants of the yeomen who founded Virginia
and made her great. Raymond Robins was poor, miserable, and
deprived as a youth. He went into wild mining regions to bring
law, order, and religion to the untutored. After that, he worked
for children's welfare groups, and was, at the time Nock's article
about him appeared, a labor agitator who, while being a radical,
"knows that the world does not change its habits of thought in
one man's lifetime, and so he is very patient, and always willing
to consider the next best thing."[20] Brand Whitlock, Nock's close
friend, was spoken of as a man who "has just one political and
social principle—he believes in the Kingdom of Heaven as a
working fact. He thinks the Sermon on the Mount, taken liter-
ally, is the final law of community life, of collective as well as
individual action."[21] Ralph Whitfield Chandless was the progressive Horatio Alger: from poor beginnings, one is expected by
thrift, hard work, and devotion to duty to emerge a great man,
because he has "the stuff." In the Jeffersonian world, success was
a thing to be earned by the practice of the laissez-faire ethic.
When success was attained, and even while it was being attained, one was expected to be a model of Christian charity, humility, and public service—virtues not well-known for their
place in the laissez-faire tradition. Success had to be earned, and
it had its responsibilities. *Noblesse oblige* was married to survival
of the fittest. The stern faith of John Winthrop had been replaced
by the pious entreaties of Andrew Carnegie.

III

Nock's attitudes during this period of experimentation thus
included a belief in the social value of Christianity, in the Chris-

tian virtues, the agrarian qualities, and in the idea of the individual striving on his own in an atmosphere of freedom, both political and economic. He was willing to try any reasonably coherent program that seemed likely to make America a more interesting, more civilized country.

The end of this period coincided with the end of the muckraking spirit in America. The movement, such as it was, appeared to be dying from success on the one hand, and frustration on the other. Steffens, a fanatical believer in the Golden Rule as the guide for a better life, took offense first at businessmen who thought the rule should apply only to others, and second at the *American* staff which tried to tone down his articles for the sake of protecting new and wealthy subscribers and advertisers. Finley Dunne began severing his connections with the *American* in the spring of 1913, although he continued to write as a contributor until the Collier interests began changing the magazine into the image of wholesome Americanism. The crisis for the muckrakers, however, was also one of money. According to Ida Tarbell, the muckrakers had become commercialized, and the public was beginning to realize it. The muckrakers were stupid, she said, for they "had lost the passion for facts in a passion for subscriptions." World War I had forced a reconsideration of basic issues and the position of the magazine. "It became a grave question whether, under the changed conditions, the increased confusion of mind, the intellectual and financial uncertainties, an independent magazine backed with little money could live." The time finally arrived when "the magazine required fresh money, and we had no more to put in. The upshot was that in 1915 the *American* was sold to the Crowell Publishing Company. The editors wanted a different type of magazine. . . ."[22]

Under the editorship of John Siddall, the *American* became a vehicle of what might be termed "factual humanism"—simply a presentation of things as they were, in the belief that this was what interested people and would cause the product to sell. Miss Tarbell, unable to continue under the new management, went into a career as a lecturer. Albert Jay Nock set sail for

Europe, on one of what became a long series of devoted pilgrimages to places where life was interesting, the capitalists not unbearably predatory, and the people capable of carrying on civilized talk.

Ray Stannard Baker, looking back after thirty years, wrote the magazine's epitaph:

It was a rare group we had there at the beginning of *The American Magazine*: men genuinely absorbed in life, genuinely in earnest in their attitude toward it, and yet with humor, and yet with sympathy, and yet with tolerance, far more eager to understand and make sure than to dream of utopias. We really believed in human beings: we really believed in democratic relationships. We "muckraked" not because we hated our world, but because we loved it. We were not hopeless, we were not cynical, we were not bitter.

Two world wars will leave little, I am afraid, of the spirit we knew in those days. The other day I reread the earliest announcement of our new magazine venture with a kind of nostalgic surprise. It couldn't have been true—it was all too naïve. But there it is in black and white, with the names of a dozen derring-do editors and authors signed to it.

"We shall not only make this new *American Magazine* interesting and important in a public way, but we shall make it the most stirring and delightful monthly book of fiction, humor, sentiment, and joyous reading that is anywhere published. It will reflect a happy, struggling, fighting world, in which, as we believe, good people are coming out on top. There is no field of human activity in which we are not interested. Our magazine will be wholesome, hopeful, stimulating, uplifting, and above all, it will have a human interest on every page, whether expressed in fiction or articles or comment or editorials."[23]

CHAPTER FOUR

THE JEFFERSONIAN AS A LIBERAL:

The Disillusionment of War, 1914–19

NOWHERE was the contrast between Nock's attitude before the war and his attitude during it more marked than in his views on pacifism. Like virtually all Jeffersonian liberals—the views of Senator Robert La Follette, Sr. and Oswald Garrison Villard, for example, were similar to Nock's—Nock was a pacifist. He believed that war or preparation for it was culturally destructive, personally degrading, and a distraction from internal improvements. Domestic reform was ignored when war broke out. But the ways in which Nock expressed these views, while the position remained unchanged, were quite different. In "World Scouts," in January, 1912, he was optimistic and just a little old-fashioned in his language. In "Peace, the Aristocrat," in May, 1915, he seemed tired, world-weary, and pessimistic.

"World Scouts" was a discussion of a new youth movement headed by Sir Francis Vane. A competitor of the Boy Scout movement, the World Scouts were to Nock a Christianizing influence, a force for civilization. The Boy Scouts, on the other hand, were "trained to believe in two artificial, false, old-fashioned and utterly exploded ideas—ideas that the world has no use for." The Boy Scout was taught first "to believe in the existence of a large class of beings called *foreigners*," and second, that it was "normal, right, and above all very glorious and interesting to oppose these beings occasionally in the institution called *warfare*." The World Scout, on the other hand, was "in these respects not trained at all. He is simply allowed and encouraged to keep the natural, true, clear vision of human beings that he was born with." To the World Scout, no such thing as a foreigner existed, and war was "neither glorious nor interesting, but, on the contrary, sordid and stupid."[1]

Rousseau would have liked this passage, and so would Jefferson. Nock assumed that people were born naturally good, and that only some unfortunate contact with a social institution defiled their basic instincts. Such a faith was necessary for philosophical anarchism, in the political sense. He assumed further that environment was the major determinant of a person's character, a faith similar to that of the educational philosophers who were working on schools that would better prepare their students for "real life."

This philosophy was a further application of the moral conviction behind the Golden Rule that motivated Steffens and the two men who had served as mayor of Toledo, Jones and Whitlock, as well as Nock. The faith was also a pragmatic one, in that it placed emphasis on beliefs that "work," or that have a tangible "cash value," to borrow a term from William James. The World Scout movement was laudable because it produced practitioners of the Golden Rule: boys who risked their lives to save people in trouble or who helped old ladies across the street, in the classically chivalrous mode. In other words, the movement worked. It channeled energies and desires into socially beneficial areas, while the Boy Scout movement was a vehicle for militarism and chauvinism.

How different was the despairing, sophisticated tone of "Peace, the Aristocrat," written less than four years later! In this article, Nock challenged the same pacifist propagandists in whose ranks he had belonged such a short time before. Peace advocates, he wrote, had a special point of view, interesting, no doubt, but beside the point. But they also had a presupposition which was little understood: "that of the rationalist philosopher or propagandist, which assumes that men are governed chiefly, or at least much more than they actually are, by reason and logic." The peace advocates were quite happy to rest their case by showing how irrational, illogical, and costly war was, assuming that such a policy would cause men to "forsake war and militarism forthwith." In actuality, "men are very little governed by reason and logic; and this accounts for the fact that in an issue between the philosopher and the politician, the politician always wins." In other words, peace advocates should stop trying to persuade men that war was evil. "What they should realize was that, to most men, war was more interesting than the dull boredom of their peacetime lives. It had pageantry and a sense of purpose; it offered men advancement by merit and heroism, not through favoritism; many of these things were next to impossible for the average American to find in peacetime."[2]

Two basic presuppositions were behind Nock's arguments. First, he believed that the way to influence the course of events was through persuasion of the minds of the intellectuals, as opposed to the propagandizing of the masses, which he thought useless. Men of thought should influence the intelligent men of action, and through the latter progress would be made. Second, Nock leaned heavily on the works and methods of Charles Beard, later a good friend. Not patriotism, but boredom and the chance of advancement were motives; intellectual conviction had little effect on most men, while whims and self-interest had a great deal. Illuminating all of Nock's work was his ultimate concern for the good life; this concern was always at the heart of his writings, and the good life became the utopia for which he constantly worked.[3] Thus when the war broke out, he could write: "Nowhere, broadly speaking, does the common man enlist because he loves war, but because he hates peace." Logically, then, the function "of the true peace advocate is not to deplore war, but to help make peace interesting. . . ."[4]

The First World War was the overwhelming presence which killed American innocence. Nock was not alone in his dismay at the sight of such a senseless conflict. The quaint virtues that Ray Stannard Baker had recorded seemed no defense against such uncontrollable events. "However the war came politically," Carl Van Doren has noted, "it came morally as an unexpectedly ghastly wound. First the shock and the stunned numbness." In his diary, Van Doren had recorded no mention of the events leading to war until July 30. Then he wrote: "The thought in my mind from morning till night was the thought of a general European war. The cataclysm has laid a hand on every soul I met today." Following the shock came incredulity, the outrage that such things were possible in a good world. "Then the horror of pain, the gradual sense that it must somehow be borne, the long endurance, fevers that rose and fell in the blood, relief and dragging recovery." But the war had done its work. "The first day of the war was the end of an illusion by which my contemporaries had lived. This was not a world of humane and reasonable order finally arrived at. This was a world in which anything still might happen."[5]

At the outbreak of the war, most liberals wished to have no part in it. Some of the more conservative, like Willard Straight or Colonel House, were openly pro-British in sympathy, if not to the point of combat. The remainder ranged to the opposite extreme of the doctrinaire Marxists, like Max Eastman, who regarded all wars as capitalist, imperialist, and evil. Soon, five interrelated but distinguishable attitudes developed among these liberals.

The pragmatists—Dewey, Croly, and Lippmann—insisted on being neither for nor against the war, but on judging by immediately attainable ends whether American intervention would be a greater good than American abstention. Eventually, they produced the vaguely comic term "Aggressive Pacifism" to justify their acceptance of Norman Angell's limited war policy.[6] A second group might be termed "moralistic." Originally pacifists, these men—President Wilson, Rabbi Wise, and occasionally a *New Republic* man, such as Walter Weyl, who was uncomfortable as a Bull Moose nationalist—ultimately decided upon intervention because of the moral import of America's opportunity to dictate a just peace and establish a League of Nations. The third group, the doctrinaire socialists, were originally the most vociferous of the pacifists. Couching their platforms in the

Masses jargon of class struggle and capitalism, these men, typi-
fied by Floyd Dell and Max Eastman, opposed all war, regardless of purpose. Shortly after their trial on sedition charges for
their views, however, events in Russia led them to an abrupt
about-face, and they served war willingly enough thereafter, as
a service to the new Slavic mecca.[7] The fourth and fifth groups
were the two variations on the traditionally liberal theme. Many
men might be classified in both groups, the distinction between
which is mainly one of language. The fourth group based its
opposition to war on the grounds that war was partly the result
of economic greed, but primarily of diplomatic conniving. It
was nothing more or less than one of the fruits of diplomacy,
and of no concern to the individual citizen. Most single taxers,
with their inevitable distrust of the state, were in this category,
notably Francis Neilson and Nock. The fifth position was that of
men such as Villard, Harold Stearns, and Randolph Bourne, who
used the language of classical liberalism. War was evil to these
men because it debauched man and civilization, it distracted
attention from internal reform, and never accomplished anything positive.

The fourth and fifth groups had their first major break with
the Hamiltonian school of the *New Republic* over the issue of intervention. A schism had occurred in 1912, but nothing that
could not be patched up by common opposition to an apparent
Tory like Charles Evans Hughes; such opposition led most liberals to support Wilson in 1916. The war reopened the break.
In the twenties, some reunion took place when most members of
the first two groups regretted the results of their actions during
the war in the disgust prevalent after Versailles. Nevertheless,
much bitterness persisted, and Wilson's violence toward his
former friends left a deep wound.

To a large degree, the difference between Hamiltonian and
Jeffersonian methods led to the split. Those who favored American emergence as an important power and her adoption of a
centralized government preferred pragmatism to rigid moral
standards as a means of achieving these ends. Those who cared

little about America's role in world politics saw their Jeffersonian ideals trampled under in the war, and pictured American entrance as a violation of the principles of the mystic past that Nock and others had created in the muckraking days. Witness, for instance, Villard's despairing reaction to the declaration of war: "It came nearer to unmanning me than anything in my life. For I knew, as I knew that I lived, that this ended the republic as we had known it; that henceforth we Americans were to be part and parcel of world politics, rivalries, jealousies, and militarism; that hate, prejudice, and passion were now enthroned in the United States."[8] Gone was American innocence, isolation, purity. Woodrow Wilson ate the European apple, and America became involved with the evil of the world.

Nock shared these feelings of violated innocence. When, in March, 1910, he wrote about Brand Whitlock and the Golden Rule, the tone was one of serene optimism: it *was* possible for men to act morally, if only they were educated for it. When the time came to write the introduction to the first edition of Whitlock's autobiography, the war clouds loomed, and for the first time Nock sensed the idea of superfluity which later haunted him and gave him the central theme for his autobiography. The artist, the sensitive man, really had no place in a world of war and materialism. He was superfluous as far as such a society and its members were concerned. The pessimism of his later years was now present, although not overwhelmingly; even so, the spirit of the piece differed greatly from the buoyancy of pre-war years. It marked the transition from experimentalism to disillusion, still containing elements of both. The best part of Whitlock's book, Nock wrote, was "the most admirable and impressive picture" which the author had unconsciously drawn of himself. "It reveals once more that tragedy—the most profound, most common and most neglected of all the multitude of useless tragedies that our weak and wasteful civilization by sheer indifference permits—the tragedy of a richly gifted nature denied the opportunity of congenial self-expression." Material deprivation was immaterial beside it. "The author is an artist, a born artist," and his true place "is in a world unknown and undreamed of by us children of an age commissioned to carry out the great idea of industrial and political development. He belongs by birthright in the eternal realm of divine impossibilities, of sublime and delightful inconsistencies."[9] Is it unfair to say that where Whitlock really belonged was in a small white house next door to Monticello? The war produced, in such men as Whitlock and Nock, the outraged innocence of people who find themselves in a world where evil has become accepted and inevitable, and who feel the frustration of their own inadequate attempts to meet and overcome the threats.

In the year between the publication of Whitlock's book and the appearance of Francis Neilson's *How Diplomats Make War*, for which Nock also wrote a preface, Nock's outrage turned into a cold, calm opposition to the conditions of a war world. For the first time his writings took on the objective, impersonal character that later became so marked. No longer did he concern himself very much with local events. Most of his attention was focused on more important, even abstract problems. The war had wrought much of this change. Perhaps his trips to Europe as an agent of William Jennings Bryan had widened his perspective. The great enthusiasm of the early *American Magazine* had evaporated when few problems were solved. His language here was sharp and biting, his style incisive, if a little old-fashioned, and his comments given with unshakable certainty.

"We are sick," he wrote, "of sham and sop, of guff and sanctimony, of oily volubility about liberty and humanity and decency and God and democracy and all the rest of it."[10] What Neilson's book offered was an immensely detailed account of the machinations of diplomats and the foreign offices of most of the European nations, particularly of Britain. Its turgid style did not much detract from the scope of its indictment of all diplomats. The thesis of the book was that "It is not a person, or some one particular Power, that was responsible for this war. It was a system that brought it about; and that system was secret diplomacy."[11] The work of later historians supported many of Neilson's opinions. The governments not the people were responsible, and the British were as guilty as the Austrians. As Nock wrote, the book showed that what Americans were being asked to sympathize with was not the people, "but with the officeholders; with the machinations and misfeasances of a baker's dozen of men who by deviltry and chicane and compromise and all the devious ways of the professional 'statesmen,' get into office and make up governments."

In league with the diplomats were the predatory interests—the descendants of the malefactors of great wealth who were the targets of the progressives: "It is a humiliating and melancholy reflection that if Congress should simply nationalize the manufacture of armaments and propose paying for them by a small tax on incomes and inheritances, we would never hear another word about 'preparedness' as long as we live—except from a few who are professionally interested, like General Wood and Mr. Roosevelt."[12]

Neilson's book, however, dealt only with Europe, and Nock attempted to apply it in America. The thesis of the book was true enough, as far as it went, but it was not sufficiently inclusive. Surely economics, misunderstanding, and sheer historical accident also helped to cause the war. It was difficult, too, to picture statesmen evil enough or strong enough to start a world war. This doctrine, like previous ones held by the progressives, smacked of the honest man who, because he was unable to control his fate, attempted to console himself by attacking those who seemed to have usurped power over men's destinies. Apparently a frustrated and unhappy man himself, Neilson had emigrated from his war-crazy country just before the book's publication. Shortly he knew further disgust, as Wilson, the man who had kept America out of war, became convinced of his mission to rescue the old world from its sinful self, blithely unaware of the fact that war was not the path to civilization or democracy.

The other great lack in Neilson's interpretation of the war—an understandable one since his book was written several years before Wilson began his moral crusading—was in his understanding of the moral reasons for men fighting. Even if America as a whole believed the thesis of the book, the moral pressure Wilson applied could have swayed them by the argument that only by fighting could the innocent, disinterested United States put a stop to such diplomatic conniving when peace came. Only a strongly documented outline of the failure of righteous wars of the past might have done this. Neilson did not provide such an argument.

One thing the book did do was to outline the liberal–radical beliefs which Neilson, Nock, Villard, and others held. The old, optimistic liberalism was mixed with the newer pessimism, which eventually prevailed. The period of transition between them has appeared puzzling out of context, for it seems to present the student with two opposing views. On the one hand, man is still capable of rationally controlling his world and improving it; on the other, forces of evil oppose man, and the brightness of the future is not assured. Hope was now giving way to hard fact, and while these liberals realized that what they saw did not correspond with what they wished, they could make the transition only slowly, and with difficulty.

Neilson first stated the liberal premise—that nations could improve only themselves, and only internally. No one could impose ideal conditions on a nation incapable of imposing them on itself. Here the split between Wilsonian moralism and liberal pacifism was sharply outlined; the question which now had to be answered was how to prevent another war. The first step was to find out what caused this war. The second was to realize that the only reform a nation could attempt was reform of itself. A corollary belief was the reliance placed on personal Christianity. Both Nielson and Nock had great use for God and the Bible, and very little for organized religion. Just as the organized elements of society were undesirable, so were the organized elements of the church.[13]

One reason why Neilson's book has remained a useful document is the accuracy of his predictions: he emphasized that the attempt to reform Europe would fail, and even corrupt those who tried, and he thought a second world war a likely aftereffect. But prediction was not his main concern. He wished to prevent further disaster. He demanded an end to secret diplomacy, and a law requiring all treaties and commitments to be passed only after public hearing in Parliament. Such conditions—echoes of the Manchester version of classical, liberal thought—were not to be considered a cure-all, but necessary first steps. "Some reduction in armaments might then be made; but let it not be imagined that these changes will be sufficient to preclude the probability. They will only give the people a chance to know what is taking place, and, perhaps, let them have more time to think before they engage in war. No more can truthfully be said in their favor."[14]

Neilson analyzed war feeling in economic terms, in contrast to Nock's view that war was really just more interesting than peace. Neilson believed that the stomach was more important than the mind in creating the willingness to fight, and so his remedy was based on the program of internal improvements which had been under way at the start of war and had been abandoned: "Yes, it is hunger, lack of a home, of decent clothes, of means of keeping clean, which are the chief reasons for men joining the ranks."[15] The only cure for war was to provide equal opportunity for every man at home. Each nation should tend to itself and its own people. Each person should take care of himself. Thus the Jeffersonian liberalism of Nock joined the Manchester liberalism of Neilson in opposition to the crusading liberalism of Wilson, the nationalism and socialism of Croly and Lippmann, and the communism of Eastman and Dell. The divergent paths of liberalism had become distinct.

II

Nock's writing pace slowed during the war. He traveled through Europe during 1914 and 1915, and throughout America when he returned. His reputation established, he could pick and choose editorial jobs, and after some free-lance work for *Century* magazine on prohibition and the ever-reappearing land question, and two distinguished articles for the *North American Review*, he accepted an invitation to join Oswald Garrison Villard's revivified *Nation*.

The essays for the *North American Review* were the finest Nock wrote during the first decade of his public career. In style and substance, they were equal to all but the very best that he produced in the next twenty years. Despite their topical nature— both concerned prohibition—they were the first extended attempts Nock made to put down his ideas about civilization. Previous articles had hinted at these ideas in passing, but only as vaguely defined goals, not as specific objects of attention.

Although claiming to be an absolute teetotaler himself at this time, Nock took prohibitionists to task rather severely. He went to Kansas, where prohibition was in force, examined what he saw, and then predicted what would happen if prohibition were extended throughout the country. Had America listened to his warning, the Noble Experiment would never have taken place.

Kansas, in abolishing her saloons, had opened up vast areas for graft, corruption, and bootlegging, and had changed the drinking habits of her people from light wines and beer to hard liquor—since the difficulty of obtaining drinks forced people to get as much alcohol as they could from a given bottle. The true evil was not liquor or drunkenness; it was absolutism. Kansas, he wrote, "has repeated the history of every absolutist enterprise since the world began," and the unprejudiced observer must come to the conclusion that the cure of prohibition was worse than the disease of drink. One asked himself whether, "after all, the open saloon would not be almost a fair exchange for the reaction produced upon any society by this kind of thing, by the perjury induced, the encouragement of furtive habits, the general spirit of fraud, deceit and hypocrisy, the abeyance of personal responsibility."[16] Nock's position was a logical development from the liberal principles of earlier years. One could not coerce people into sobriety any more than one could coerce them into peace. But the country felt otherwise, as it had during the war.

The real point of the essays, however, was not the effectiveness of prohibition. It was whether prohibition contributed to civilization and the good life. "The question is not whether prohibition prohibits, but whether, under prohibition, the general civilization is such as 'a well-formed mind would be disposed to relish.'"[17] Prohibition failed the test. Not only did it create the undesirable conditions already outlined, it also made it difficult for people in Kansas to develop a sense of right and wrong. New York children, Nock said pointedly, may grow up next door to a saloon, but at least they are exposed to the necessity for choice and valuation. "The chief point is that New York children may grow up with a just sense of moral values, in this particular, while Kansas children may not."[18] In other words, New York children, by facing corruption under the guidance of their families and teachers, could learn to handle it. Kansas children had to grow up in a make-believe world in which evil was apparently banished, but in which, in reality, it grew deeper since it was under cover and there was no one trained to combat it.

Always keeping in view the good life, Nock then outlined his solution to the problem. Wine and beer, he felt, were valuable and enjoyable additions to civilized life, and produced few alcoholics; hard liquor was less defensible. The solution was the system he had seen operating in Norway that summer (1916). There the issue of reform, not of revenue or coercion, was paramount. The Norwegians believed that light wines, beer, and cider contributed to the good life, and therefore they taxed these beverages lightly, if at all. Such drinks were common, and their sale was not restricted to licensed outlets. Hard liquor, however, was regarded with suspicion and highly taxed. It was not prohibited; rather it was made so expensive that most people simply could not afford it. The fact that it could still be obtained meant that bootlegging was unprofitable. Thus corruption and graft did not endanger the good life, and the availability of mild intoxicants produced few alcoholics. Norwegians could have their pleasure, could spend their tax money, and best of all, they could develop moral values in a civilization that "a well-formed mind would be disposed to relish."[19]

Nock's career on the *Nation* was brief and not notably distinguished. Villard spoke of him with great respect, however,[20] and Nock probably did a great deal of editing and editorializing along with his occasional typical articles. But he did little of note for future generations. The one brief flurry of comment that did occur to Nock came during the war, when he wrote the editorial on Samuel Gompers which the bureaucrats in the Post Office Department—notably the postmaster general, Albert Burleson, and his solicitor, William H. Lamar—took as an excuse for banning that issue of the magazine. As Lamar said, Gompers had kept labor in line for Wilson, and they were not going to stand by and see him insulted. Simply another example of the willingness of men in Wilson's administration to use the confusion of war to impose their prejudices on America by force, the incident only convinced both Nock and Villard of the disastrous effects of war. A. Mitchell Palmer was soon to prove their case in his attempts to keep America clean. Rarely, if ever, did Wilson reprimand his subordinates or soften their actions. His decline and fall did not noticeably disturb the men on whom he had turned so bitterly in 1917.[21]

Nock finished his apprenticeship in journalism in the last minutes of the decade. No longer a completely optimistic believer in the innate goodness of man and his world, he had not learned a new vocabulary, and his writings during the next few years exhibited a curious schizophrenia to the men who read them. His disillusion with the past, however, was permanent. While Nock still idolized Jefferson and shared his goal of the good life, he displayed a mature skepticism about things which had been taken for granted, and a pessimism about the possibility of improvement. The war had taught Nock and men like him the undesirability of attempting to meddle in the affairs of others. Henceforth they concentrated on self-improvement as the only way to obtain a brighter future. Society and its leaders could point the way to improvement, could educate and lead, but the use of force was self-defeating, and brought evil both to the coercer and the coerced. The lesson of Woodrow Wilson, that evil could not be used to achieve good, had been painfully learned. Nock never forgot it, and memory of it haunted his writings throughout the rest of his career.

CHAPTER FIVE

INTELLECTUAL FOUNDATIONS:

Matthew Arnold, Herbert Spencer,
Henry George, Franz Oppenheimer

Nock's Jeffersonian upbringing, with its egalitarian, self-reliant characteristics, confirmed his predispositions and made him a follower of Jefferson. Although in spirit a member of the Jeffersonian tradition, Nock took the great majority of his political, social, and historical ideals from sources different from, if not incompatible with, Jeffersonian democracy. He had been a teacher in a minor way, a clergyman, a journalist, and a polemicist. During and after the war, while on the *Nation* (1918–19), Nock rounded out his education. His early education had been in a strict classical curriculum, and by his own admission this included virtually nothing of world affairs after 1500. The faith he finally found and began to articulate in his own magazine in 1920 was based in large part on the works of four nineteenth-century theorists: Matthew Arnold, Henry George, Herbert Spencer, and Franz Oppenheimer. Other influences, most notably Goethe, Marx, Jefferson, Quesnay, Turgot, Cobden, Bright, John and Henry Adams, Jeremy Taylor, and even Thomas à Kempis could be noted in his work, but these four men provided the core of Nock's thought.

ii

What Jefferson meant by the "good life" Matthew Arnold called "culture." This end, as I have stressed, was always Nock's ultimate purpose. But only in his earlier days did Nock endorse many of Arnold's means and methods for obtaining this end. Rather than using the state as the instrument of the best self in humanity, as Arnold did in his defense of the established church in *Culture and Anarchy,* Nock turned to the opposite pole, represented by Herbert Spencer, one of the staunch liberals whom Arnold attacked at such length in his essay. Spencer, in the first edition of the *Social Statics* and in the essays later collected in *The Man vs. the State,* set forth the doctrines which were to dominate liberal thought in England for generations and which, even before *On the Origin of the Species,* heralded the approach of the social Darwinism that grew to be so influential in American circles. Spencer, furthermore, pointed out the issue of land possession and monopoly that Henry George seized upon and elucidated in his work of economic theory, *Progress and Poverty,* whose effect on Nock and the progressives I have already noted. Finally, twenty years after George published his work, an obscure German sociologist and political theorist, Franz Oppenheimer, began work on a theory of the state based on an economic interpretation of history, and on the earlier sociological research of Gumplowicz, Ratzenhofer, and Ratzel. His book, published in America in 1908 as *The State (Der Staat),* gave historical basis for the dislike of governmental institutions which was ever-present in the work of Spencer and George. These four books may be examined in Nock's own light, taking what he took to form a viable social philosophy.

III

In 1869, England was in a state of change. The liberals, under Bright and Gladstone, were attempting to enfranchise more voters and to disestablish the Anglican Church. Part of *Culture and Anarchy,* indeed, was nothing more than a campaign pamphlet in the 1868 elections. But Arnold had more enduring problems on his mind. The book was a wholesale onslaught against dissident religion, the perils of "doing as one likes," and the faith

in machinery which characterized most liberals and their followers. More important, it was a statement of values which influenced criticism of all sorts for years to come.

Culture was Arnold's concern, and he conceived it to be "a pursuit of our total perfection by means of getting to know . . . the
best which has been thought and said in the world." In other
words, "it is a study of perfection."[1] The way to achieve such a
state was through the exercise of an established state religion.
Religion to Arnold was "the greatest and most important of the
efforts by which the human race has manifested its impulse to
perfect itself." Religion was the inseparable companion of culture in the effort to "ascertain what perfection is and to make it
prevail." Religion taught that "*The kingdom of God is within
you*; and culture, in like manner, places human perfection in an
internal condition, in the growth and predominance of our humanity proper, as distinguished from our animality."[2]

The essence of this spirit of religion was a felicitous union of
what Arnold called Hebraism, or strictness of conscience, and
Hellenism, or spontaneity of consciousness. His England, he felt,
had too much Hebraism and too little Hellenism, and his emphasis on culture was an attempt to place these two instincts in better proportion. The state, to Arnold, was the ideal mate for religion since "the state is of the religion of all its citizens without the
fanaticism of any of them."[3] It was, in other words, an expression
of the best self of all the people.

Besides his emphasis on culture and Hellenism—two themes
which were of great importance to Nock—Arnold made a crucial
distinction which influenced Nock greatly in the decade before
he died. This distinction was the famous one between barbarians,
philistines, and populace, on the one hand, and the idea of *humanity* on the other. The uncultured upper class were the barbarians, the uncultured middle class the philistines, and the uncultured lower class the populace. The importance of this classification lay in Arnold's separating a certain few from each of
these groups, with no regard for economic status, for his humanity. The idea was quite in keeping with Jefferson's élite. As

Arnold stated his theory: in "each class there are born a certain number of natures with a curiosity about their best self, with a bent for seeing things as they are, for disentangling themselves from machinery, for simply concerning themselves with reason and the will of God, and doing their best to make these prevail; —for the pursuit, in a word, of perfection."[4]

Arnold's views seemed to influence Nock in their entirety during his career in the clergy. His endorsement of state action during the *American Magazine* years—not to mention Jack Reed's doggerel—indicated that he subscribed to many of them even after he left the active ministry. The two important ideas he retained from Arnold were the idea of culture as the attainment of perfection, and the notion of the élite humanity. Both ideas were perfectly in harmony with the Jeffersonian tradition. The ideas he eventually discarded, on religion, and the state as the expression of the best self of a population, were significantly at variance with this tradition.

IV

Nock and the liberal tradition owed their greatest debts to Herbert Spencer. Oddly enough it was his early work, and not his later synthetic philosophy and its increasing conservatism, that had greatest influence. Indeed, one of the most influential parts of the *Social Statics*, the part dealing with monopoly in land, Spencer explicitly rejected later; he even went to the extreme of completely forbidding an unrevised reprint of the first edition while he lived.

The argument of this book began with the premise that "human happiness is the divine will."[5] "Happiness" is defined as "a gratified state of all the faculties,"[6] the gratification being produced by the exercise of the faculties to an appropriate degree. Spencer then postulated a "moral sense" contained by every individual, and cited evidence that humanity was indefinitely variable. Because of this variability, humanity could not be used as a gauge for testing moral truth. Nature, however, was invariable, and its rules "have no exceptions. The apparent ones are only apparent, not real. They are indications either that we have not found the true law or that we have got an imperfect expression of it."[7]

Spencer's vision of human development might be pictured in a diagram in which a straight line (nature's unchanging law throughout history) is intersected at some distant point (the state of perfection) by a line from below. This line (the human race's ever-improving moral and social nature) was originally far removed from the line of perfection, but inevitable progress and the weeding out of unsuitable beings were slowly bringing the millennium nearer. All that happened was guided by an inscrutable but good Providence. Every event had meaning and was somehow good, and its apparent evil was but a fault in the vision of the imperfect viewer.

Spencer erected his moral philosophy on the first line, the perfect one toward which man was striving, since to him it was ridiculous to base an absolute moral code on a changing and imperfect humanity. Because his system treated "abstract principles of right conduct," it could not "recognize evil or any of those conditions which evil generates. It entirely ignores wrong, injustice, or crime, and gives no information as to what must be done when they have been committed." No infractions of law were permitted, since only a statement of the law was attempted. He said, then, that "such-and-such are the principles on which men should act, and when these are broken it can do nothing but say they *are* broken."[8]

Evil, in such a system, "results from the non-adaptation of constitution to conditions."[9] It was, in other words, the gap between the two lines in my diagram, ever-present but gradually closing up in a world where man was expected to approach perfection. Thus the social state and the moral law, the actual and the ideal, coexisted at wide but constantly decreasing variance throughout history.

In a historical sense, Spencer's application of this world view was more important than his derivation of it. Nock and others had rejected, implicitly if not explicitly, the doctrine of inevitable human perfectability by the time the *Freeman* was born, but they had not rejected Spencer's application. They took instead Arnold's view of the study of perfection and the realization of the best self in humanity and said that Spencer's means were the best method of obtaining this end. Spencer's social views were similar to those held by thinkers in the tradition of Jefferson and Henry George, and were assimilated by them with little trouble. In fact, the great success which Spencer's later, conservative social doctrines—as well as the Synthetic Philosophy—enjoyed in this country is evidence that the Jeffersonian tradition had prepared the foundation for such a set of beliefs. Significantly, Spencer was far more popular in America than he was in England.

To Spencer, man's dilemma was how to obey a perfect moral law in an imperfect world. From this problem, Spencer produced the principle that was but a reformulation of much that had been thought before, but which had never been given a respectable philosophical foundation. "In this social state," Spencer wrote, "the sphere of activity of each individual being limited by the spheres of activity of other individuals, it follows that the men who are to realize this greatest sum of happiness must be men of whom each can obtain complete happiness within his own sphere of activity without diminishing the spheres of activity required for the acquisition of happiness by others."[10] In other words, if it were God's will that men be happy, and this happiness could be achieved only through the exercise of his faculties, then God willed that man exercise his faculties. This exercise presupposed freedom of action, a freedom which should be bounded only by the similar freedom of all. The state's sole duty was to maintain conditions making such a state of freedom possible. The first principle of the *Social Statics* was: "Every man has freedom to do all that he wills, provided he infringes not the equal freedom of any other man."[11] Ever since, this has been the rallying cry of liberals in the Spencerian tradition, whether they be called radicals, anarchists, conservatives, or whatever. The statement, sometimes attributed to the legendary King Pausole as "hurt no man, then do as you will," or to Rabelais as the motto of the Abbey of Thélème, reoccurred constantly throughout Nock's writings. To him, it indicated the only means of attaining that study of perfection that Arnold, and Jefferson before him, regarded as the proper goal of man.

In the application of his principle, Spencer was unflinching. He opposed practically every state function, from sanitation to charity, and when he could find something for the state to do, such as mail delivery, he demanded the privilege of private mail operation as a goad to quality and speed. Each individual has the right to life, personal property, use of the land, and so on. Indeed, "government is essentially immoral," since it had its origin in the evil area between human experience and the perfection of the moral law. As evil gradually disappeared from the earth, so too would government, since its presence could be justified only by evil. In the meantime, evil government was necessary. Of all governments, "a purely democratic government is the only one which is morally admissible," since it was the only one with the ethically necessary principle of voluntarism.

Basic, too, to the Spencerian theory was the idea of perfection as an internal sentiment. Evidence of Nock's devotion to this idea could be found throughout the pages of the *Freeman*. External conditions mattered little if the inner man were faulty. The drawing out of this inner sentiment is another way of expressing the goal of the *Freeman*: "Political freedom, therefore, is as we say, an external result of an inner sentiment—is alike, in origin, practicability, and permanence, dependent on the moral sense; and it is only when this is supreme in its influence that so high a form of social organization as a democracy can be maintained."[12] It is difficult to see how Matthew Arnold could have quarreled with such a sentiment. The two might conceivably have disagreed about the ultimate perfectability of man, or his status in the nineteenth century, but the desirability of inner perfection was a major point with both writers.

V

Henry George's *Progress and Poverty* was an extension into economics of Spencer's right to the use of the earth. What George was trying to do, in a historical sense, was "to unite the truth perceived by the school of Smith and Ricardo to the truth perceived by the school of Proudhon and Lassalle; to show that *laissez faire* (in its full true meaning) opens the way to a realization of the noble dreams of socialism. . . ."[13] George lived in speculation-ridden California in a time of wild boom and bust, and the book grew directly out of his experience. Despite constant efforts at work, and willingness to do virtually anything, George found himself without money, and with a wife and children. His despair at this situation set him to thinking, and *Progress and Poverty* was the most successful result. The problem was simply stated: "Where the conditions to which material progress everywhere tends are most fully realized—that is to say, where population is densest, wealth greatest, and the machinery of production and exchange most highly developed—we find the deepest poverty, the sharpest struggle for existence, and the most of enforced idleness."[14]

Much of the introduction to the book was devoted to a refutation of the Malthusian dogma, then current, which is of little concern for this book, and a discussion and definition of terms. This latter was of great importance. In their briefest, clearest statement, these important definitions were:

> Land, labor and capital are the factors of production. The term land includes all natural opportunities or forces; the term labor, all human exertion; and the term capital, all wealth used to produce more wealth. In returns to these three factors is the whole produce distributed. That part which goes to land owners as payment for the use of natural opportunities is called rent; that part which constitutes the reward of human exertion is called wages; and that part which constitutes the return for the use of capital is called interest.

These terms mutually exclude each other. The income of any individual may be made up from any one, two, or all three of these sources; but in the effort to discover the laws of distribution we must keep them separate.[15]

Rent, of course, was the bugaboo which George made famous. It was "the price of monopoly, arising from the reduction to individual ownership of natural elements which human exertion can neither produce nor increase." The rent of land was determined by "the excess of its produce over that which the same application can secure from the least productive land in use." And, since men tended to satisfy their needs by the least possible exertion, he who could live on rent not only would not work, he would live off the work of others.

The area which suffered under high rent was that of wages, which depended upon the margin of production, or "upon the produce which labor can obtain at the highest point of natural productiveness open to it without the payment of rent."[16] Logically, therefore, the problem was solved. Progress and poverty increased proportionately because "the value of land depending wholly upon the power which its ownership gives of appropriating wealth created by labor, the increase of land values is always at the expense of the value of labor. And, hence, that the increase of productive power does not increase wages, is because it does increase the value of land. Rent swallows up the whole gain and pauperism accompanies progress."[17]

George's plan had the beauty, simplicity, shortness, and radicalism of ideal panacea: "We must make land common property." He deduced it from a notion of natural rights: it was, he claimed, "a right proclaimed by the fact of [men's] existence," since it cannot be assumed that some men would be granted rights and others not by a good God. Unlike Spencer, however, George would not compensate those who might suffer under such an abrupt change in social administration. A wrong was a wrong to George, even unto the seventh generation, and he specifically rejected Spencer's less radical view in his discussion of the issue. Here, too, George's doctrine bore a great similarity to Marxist theory, even though specifically rejecting the class theory and the violent revolution: "Historically, as ethically, private property in land is robbery. It nowhere springs from contract; it can nowhere be traced to perceptions of justice or expediency; it has everywhere had its birth in war and conquest, and in the selfish use which the cunning have made of superstition and law."[18]

In practice, however, George was not as violent as he might have sounded. What he really demanded was not wholesale upheaval and confiscation, but a viable principle for operation. For once the title of land had passed to the state, and the state was considered landlord and all men tenants, the administration of the single tax was simple. "What is necessary for the use of the land," George wrote, "is not its private ownership, but the security of improvements." One did not have to tell a man, "this land is yours," in order to have him work it; one had to say only, "whatever your labor or capital produces on this land shall be yours." In other words, "Give a man security that he may reap, and he will sow; assure him of the possession of the house he wants to build, and he will build it." The ownership of the land had "nothing to do with it."[19]

Thus all the state would have to do was abolish all taxation except that on land values—the single tax. George claimed that his policy, "*to appropriate rent by taxation,*" would cure just about everything. It would, he wrote, "raise wages, increase the earnings of capital, extirpate pauperism, abolish poverty, give remunerative employment to whoever wishes it, afford free scope to human powers, lessen crime, elevate morals, and taste, and intelligence, purify government and carry civilization to yet nobler heights. . . ."[20]

Whatever its more grandiose claims, the single tax was quite consciously formulated as an expression of the Jeffersonian tradition, including the *Social Statics.* "Society would thus approach the ideal of Jeffersonian democracy, the promised land of Herbert Spencer, the abolition of government,"[21] George wrote.

But a new note had been added, for even while Spencer was putting the finishing touches on the various volumes of his *Synthetic Philosophy*, with its calm certainty of the upward spiral of man toward perfection, George introduced the cyclical idea of history. George's pessimism and not Spencer's optimism eventually prevailed in liberal minds: "It is not merely an isolated case that thus confronts the theory—*it is the universal rule*. Every civilization that the world has yet seen has had its period of vigorous growth, or arrest and stagnation; its decline and fall. Of all the civilizations that have arisen and flourished, there remain today but those that have been arrested, and our own, which is not yet as old as were the pyramids when Abraham looked upon them—while behind the pyramids were twenty centuries of recorded history."[22] Like Marx, George felt that the adoption of his scheme would end this historical pattern, assuming, one supposes, that history automatically stopped with the attainment of equality. Association in equality was the law of progress to George, and without it civilizations were doomed.

Like most radical writers, George seemed to have a far greater gift for analysis and criticism than for construction of an alternative solution. The same is true of Spencer and Arnold. Spencer's analysis of the faults of utilitarian theory was accurate to the point of devastation, and his later analyses in *The Man vs. the State* were equally perceptive. Arnold's criticism of Spencer, Bright, and Bentham (no one seems to have had much respect for Bentham) was just as perceptive and telling. Yet few of his readers have been converted to belief in an established church as an instrument of achieving humanity and the realization of one's best self. Thus the logical prediction might be that Nock would turn out to be a sharply perceptive critic, and a relatively inferior constructor of substitutes. And so it has turned out.

VI

Unlike the other three men, who played such decisive roles in Nock's development, Dr. Franz Oppenheimer was never a celebrated hero with a large following. Nevertheless, this professor of political science at the University of Frankfurt-am-Main contributed important doctrines to the movement. Using the historical approach to newly formulated sociological and economic data, Oppenheimer arrived at conclusions that would have satisfied both George and Spencer, and horrified Matthew Arnold.

Every state, Oppenheimer wrote, "has been and is a class state, and every theory of the state has been and is a class theory"; every state in history "was or is a *state of classes*, a polity of superior and inferior social groups, based upon distinctions either of rank or of property." Thus the state "may be defined as an organization of *one class* dominating over the other classes." Society was that portion of the community which was opposed to the state, the non-exploiting voluntary association for which George and Spencer had so much praise. It was "the totality of concepts of all purely natural relations and institutions between man and man, which will not be fully realized until the last remnant of the creations of the barbaric 'ages of conquest and migration' has been eliminated from community life."[23]

Like George and the early Spencer, Oppenheimer was concerned with the land as an instrument of exploitation. For, he reasoned, since the land has never been completely settled economically, the lack of it for those willing to toil can only be explained by its political pre-emption. Thus the state "can have originated in no other way than through conquest and subjugation. Therefore, Oppenheimer was ready to state the thesis of his book, a thesis which did much to explain the resistance of the radicals to virtually any state activity:

> The state, completely in its genesis, essentially and almost completely during the first stages of its existence, is a social institution, forced by a victorious group of men on a defeated group, with the sole purpose of regulating the dominion of the victorious group over the vanquished, and securing itself against revolt from within and attacks from abroad. Teleologically, this dominion has no other purpose than the economic exploitation of the vanquished by the victors.[24]

This definition was one vital contribution to radical thought. A second one, equal if not greater in importance, was the closely related distinction between the "economic means" and the "political means." Man had certain desires which he wished to satisfy, postulated Oppenheimer, and his life could be interpreted as his attempts to satisfy these desires, whether aimed at food, love, or philosophy. In the operations of the world, only two means of satisfying these desires existed: work or robbery. The first method was the economic means, the second the political means. Because man sought to satisfy his needs with the least possible exertion, some would always resort to the easier method, robbery. The state was the institutionalization of the political means, and society, of the economic means. Thus world history was the story of a contest between state and society, robbery and work: "All world history, from primitive times up to our own civilization, presents a single phase, a contest namely between the economic and the political means. . . ."[25] Or, as Spencer might have said, the honest man was always against the state.

VII

Thus the radical mind: spirit and object from Matthew Arnold, philosophy and politics from Herbert Spencer, economics from Henry George, and history and sociology from Franz Oppenheimer. There were of course contradictions among these men, but then few radicals ever agree on everything. In making this rough outline of Nock's interpretation of this tradition, I have sought to organize disparate elements as an example of what one respected leader of this tradition believed. All new thought is but the rearrangement of old thought, as someone has said with some truth, and a man can rarely be original without knowing what has already been done. Nock's own peculiar synthesis was original, although few of its parts were. On these foundations he built his house.

CHAPTER SIX

THE JEFFERSONIAN AS A RADICAL:

The *Freeman* Years, 1920–24

A MERICA in the twenties was not the land of the good life. On this statement, virtually every artist, writer, and critic agreed. It was the land of the Wilson lie, of disillusionment, cynicism, and George F. Babbitt. Brave men had gone to Europe to make the world safe for democracy,

> walked eye-deep in hell
> believing in old men's lies, then unbelieving
> came home, home to a lie,
> home to many deceits and new infamy;
> usury age-old and age-thick
> and liars in public places.

They discovered that their finest members had died in vain,

> For an old bitch gone in the teeth,
> For a botched civilization.[1]

Extreme or not, Ezra Pound's outlook differed little from the outlooks of the liberals and literary men around him.

The phrase "the good life," in the previous decade only referred to in passing by most writers, was repeated with increasing frequency as writers tried to put into words their sense of isolation from the large body of Americans. The hope and optimism of the progressives had become caustic grunts of pessimism or the comic pillory that was the *American Mercury*. One of the most unhappy of the younger generation was Harold Stearns, and to him the twenties owed some sort of debt. In 1922, he produced a volume of essays, written by leading men in each of thirty fields, in which American life was outlined more searchingly, probably, than it ever had been before. The tone of *Civilization in the United States* ranged from resignation to despair. American institutions were either corrupt or grossly materialistic, and culture had little or no place except as an amusement for women. Morality had deserted public life, and all values were measured in dollars and cents.

The views presented in Stearns' book were widely held. Virtually no literary figures of note challenged them. Stearns wrote: "In no country as in the United States have the tragic consequences of the lack of any common concept of the good life been so strikingly exemplified, and in no country has the break with those common concepts been so sharp. . . . It is not that Americans make money because they love to do so, but because there is nothing else to do. . . ." America was the land not of the free but of the mindless. Aesthetic sense either had never existed, or had atrophied: ". . . the most moving and pathetic fact in the social life of America today is emotional and aesthetic starvation, of which the mania for petty regulation, the driving, regimenting, and drilling, the secret society and its grotesque regalia, the firm grasp on the unessentials of material organization of our pleasures and gaieties are all eloquent stigmata."[2]

II

The *Freeman* was a magazine founded by Nock and Neilson in 1920 to give an outlet for their peculiar political beliefs and provide a forum for new writers who might otherwise have trouble publishing. Supported by Helen Swift, Neilson's second wife, the magazine lasted through four illustrious years as an elegantly thumbed nose at the condition of the cultural life in the United States. Staff members included Nock, Neilson, Van

Wyck Brooks, Suzanne La Follette, Geroid Tanquary Robinson, Walter Fuller, and Harold Kellock. Regular contributors were John Dos Passos, Lewis Mumford, Bertrand Russell, Newton Arvin, Robert Hillyer, Mary and Padraic Colum, Louis Untermeyer, Charles Beard—the list was endless. Every week in austere pages of double-column type (the magazine was modeled on the London *Spectator*), the leading writers of the country, as Beard wrote later, "sprinkled acid on many a sacred convention," reviewed books that might have been years out of print, and pointedly ignored any appeal to mass "taste."

Neilson and Nock, the co-editors, had first met in Britain in June, 1915, through a mutual acquaintance with Brand Whitlock, then Wilson's ambassador to Belgium. After a brief stay with Neilson, Nock returned to America with the manuscript of *How Diplomats Make War*. Neilson and his first wife soon followed. Because Neilson was still a member of Parliament, his book was published anonymously. In the next three years he was divorced, and quickly married the meat heiress, Helen Swift. For two years, Neilson, his new wife, and Nock saw each other off and on. In the friendship that developed, Neilson recommended Nock's appointment to the *Nation* staff; Mrs. Neilson paid his salary there.

By the summer of 1919, however, Nock was ready to quit his *Nation* job. Disagreements over policy, to show later in his pointed attacks on the "liberal mind," as well as a desire to be his own boss were his main motivations. Mrs. Neilson agreed to subsidize the *Freeman* in an effort to give her husband something to do which would enable him to exercise his literary talents and to express his political views. Together, the three planned the policy of the *Freeman*. Nock recruited the staff. The first issue appeared on March 17, 1920.

For Nock, the experience was valuable. For four years he had the opportunity to set down his ideas, receive criticism of them, and revise them. He wrote dozens of editorials on politics, foreign affairs, aesthetics, religion, morals, education, and on virtually everything he felt worth a comment. He had not yet acquired

the highly polished style that marked his later essays. No doubt
the pressure of editorial work and the great number of his essays
contributed to their occasional lack of excellence. Nevertheless,
they were of consistently high quality, and proved to be an invaluable training for a man of letters.[3]

The good life of the Jeffersonian tradition was always the goal
of Nock's writings. Economic freedom was a means to this end;
politics was hated because it blocked the way; foreign affairs
were exercises in bankrupt thought, because they seemed based
on the lie of Versailles and had no greater aim than imperialist
aggrandizement; aesthetic standards needed reinforcement because of the deterioration of literature and the means for judging
it; and so on, through a number of less emphasized topics. Again
and again, "good life" was repeated like a litany of faith, to be
achieved only by a renunciation of the sins of political and
avaricious man.

Here the meaning of "liberal," which I noted earlier, became
particularly important. Political and economic thought in this
country has undergone deceptive changes in the past fifty years,
and words have changed their meanings. In the pre-war years,
Nock was a liberal. He called himself one, and he was called one
by others. The crossroads of liberalism marked the start of a confusing problem, which I have already outlined (Hamilton vs.
Jefferson). The result was that many people in the twenties in-
discriminately grouped all the old-style liberals under one name,
and to a great many people, the distinctions between liberals,
socialists, Communists, anarchists, and radicals were blurred un-
recognizably. Even members of these groups were themselves
confused. Nock's old friend Villard welcomed the *Freeman* cor-
dially as a liberal paper in the *Nation*. Nock himself tended to
group the more nationalistic *New Republic* with the *Nation* as
liberal, without close examination of the differing positions of
the two magazines.

The important thing for Nock and the *Freeman* was the distinction between "liberal" and "radical." To him and many
others, the conditions existing in the post-Versailles world were

the result of a failure in liberal thought. "We can not help remembering that this was a liberal's war, a liberal's peace, and that the present state of things is the consummation of a fairly long, fairly extensive, and extremely costly experiment with liberalism in political power."[4] There was considerable bitterness and disillusionment in this statement, and similar sentiments pervaded much of the political writing in the *Freeman*. The antidote to liberalism was radicalism, and the method of Nock's particular radicalism was to emphasize a change in ideas, rather than in existing institutions.

Nock was pointedly exact in his answer to the *Nation*'s welcoming editorial. After distinguishing between the nature of his magazine and that of the *Nation* and the *New Republic*, he continued with an expression of policy which was straight from Oppenheimer. "In the philosophy of public affairs," he began, "the liberal gets at his working theory of the state by the 'high priory' road; that is to say, by pure conjecture." When confronted by something like the state, the liberal would, like Carey, derive it from the action of a gang of marauders, or like Rousseau, from a social contract. Such speculations were interesting, but only speculations. "The radical gets at his theory of the State by the historical method; by tracing back and examining every appearance of the State, to the most remote examples that history can furnish. . . ."[5]

While the liberal felt, then, that the state was essentially social and improvable by political means, the radical felt that the state was essentially antisocial. Thus the only way to improve conditions was to improve the status of economic men; politics was nothing more than the economic exploitation of one class by another, an idea as much from Marx as it was from Oppenheimer. Any valuable achievement of this form of government was improbable in the light of existing conditions. The only way to improve its possibilities was to educate its subjects. As Edmund Burke wrote, in a passage Nock was particularly fond of: "If a great change is to be made in human affairs, the minds of men will be fitted to it; the general opinions and feelings will draw that way. Every fear, every hope, will forward it; and then they who persist in opposing this mighty current in human affairs, will appear rather to resist the decrees of Providence itself than the designs of men. They will not be resolute and firm, but perverse and obstinate."[6] The *Freeman*, politically, was an attempt to make most of the world feel perverse and obstinate. The mighty current did not run for another ten years. When it did, the *Freeman*, had it still been in existence, might well have had grounds for second thoughts.

Such an attitude inevitably brought accusations of snobbishness, impracticality, ineffectuality, and so on. To many, the charges were just. When pressed, Nock outlined his program for idea-moulding (but only after apoligizing for doing it). First, he wrote, "write to Washington for a copy of the Ralston-Nolan bill, now before Congress; then get a discussion of this bill and its underlying principles in every school debating society, local newspaper, women's club, Chamber of Commerce, Board of Trade, and similar bodies. . . ." Second, before these bodies, get a discussion going about "land values in the problem of housing, with special attention to determining whether land-values are by right private property in the same sense that the products of labour are private property." Third, in these same bodies, get a discussion and analysis of "the effect of the private monopoly of economic rent upon (1) wages, hours, and the conditions of labour; and upon (2) the employment of capital in industry; and analysing the effect that would be produced upon these by the abolition of such monopoly." Finally, in the same manner, discuss "agricultural land-values as a factor in the business of agriculture and in the general cost of living."[7] This was not exactly a ringing call to arms, nor was it so intended. Education in the radical truths was the *Freeman*'s aim—at least on the editorial pages.

But the break with liberalism was sharp and clear. The Jeffersonians in the twenties usually preferred the term "radical," sometimes "democrat" or "progressive." Oddly enough, the Hamiltonians, those who had rallied to Wilson on the war issue and who were internationalist in foreign affairs, had the word "liberal" to themselves. Yet in policies, the "radicals" were closer to the Manchester tradition of Cobden, Bright, and Herbert Spencer; they tended toward pacifism and free trade, and they considered themselves fighters of privilege who hated all diplomacy and felt that liberty and equality could coexist peacefully.

The bitterness and reprisal caused by the war, the inflaming of the coarser sentiments, the neglect of domestic reform, and the sheer inconsequence and opacity of much of the liberal rhetoric were singled out by Nock in his explicit statement on the rejected faith. "The failure of liberalism," he wrote harshly, "is in our judgment a failure in intelligence, in competent observation, in clear and accurate thinking; it is a failure in lucidity and logic." The liberal displayed two standard modes of unreality. "One is the unreality of incompetence and the other is the unreality of inconsequence. The first makes emotion do duty for thought, the second makes words and phrases do duty for ideas."[8]

III

Nock wrote more than twice as many essays on various aspects of diplomacy as he wrote on any other subject in the *Freeman*. Throughout, he maintained a strictly traditional Jeffersonian outlook, tempered in terminology by the economics of Henry George and the economic interpretation of history that seemed to be an amalgam of Oppenheimer, Beard, and Marx. The pacifism, distrust of politics, aversion to foreign entanglements, and antipathy toward England, which were included in this tradition, all found expression in his writings. The state, as the organization of the political means, was responsible for the war; its imperialistic desires for land, markets, and power as voiced through its diplomats—the diplomats of *How Diplomats Make War*—were the causes of the clash of economic interests which touched it off.

The confluence of such ideas in Nock's view is not unexpected.

While having no sympathy whatsoever with the techniques of communism or any other "ism" that was nothing but glorified statism, Nock had no aversion to borrowing what he felt was valuable in Marx. He even, at one point in his career, recommended a close reading of certain parts of *Das Kapital* as a kind of homage to the man who had put the notion of "economic man" in the air—the contribution of Marx which Nock felt to be most valuable. The economic interpretation of history, although presently out of favor, was an accepted technique for historians of the radical circle, and knowledge of this fact is vital to a complete understanding of the radical mind as it operated in Nock and in the *Freeman*. In its most concise expression, Nock's view was that the fundamental, general, and only cause of war was "from rivalries in economic imperialism." Such a policy was adopted by a government "as the result of the exportation of capital," which occurred when "monopoly of domestic natural resources makes it more profitable to employ capital in the development of foreign markets and enterprises than in domestic investments; and as that monopoly tightens and its price increases, the exportation of capital increases." Thus as long as monopoly control of natural resources persisted, "the exportation of capital will go on, economic imperialism will go on, and wars will recur." Perhaps in the distant future war would become so expensive that it would be abandoned as unprofitable, perhaps through a device like the League of Nations. Although the League had little affected the possibility of war, it could be looked upon as a pilot project. But as it stood, it was nothing more nor less than "a method of sustaining economic imperialism without the risk and cost of war," and as such could be regarded only as socially acceptable imperialism. As long as something could be gotten from war, Nock insisted, people would wage it. Nothing could alter this.[9]

In the context of the twenties, the only thing that might be done to redeem the world from another war was to rewrite the Treaty of Versailles. Only with a new beginning, acknowledging that both parties, not just Germany, were guilty, and that reparations and annexations were both unjustified and futile, could the age produce anything different from what might otherwise be expected. Moral pressure on Britain and France toward this aim was the only break Nock was willing to take, with his belief in the disaster of entangling alliances.[10] Probably such a scheme would not work, considering the caliber of the diplomats involved and their states' perpetual desires to maintain control of the political means. Nevertheless, only when war debts and reparations had been canceled could normal trade and economic life be restored. Only when the myth of German guilt was put down forever could the Weimar Republic be expected to act responsibly.

The major expression of these feelings was a series of articles, later republished as Nock's first book: *The Myth of a Guilty Nation.* Based on the work of Neilson and E. D. Morel, the book offered little that was new.[11] It was, however, a portent of things to come, and will always retain a minor historical importance. Harry Elmer Barnes, the man who, more than anyone else, was responsible for popularizing Nock's thesis—"that the German Government was not solely guilty of bringing on the war"[12]— has recently written of Nock and his book: *"The Myth of a Guilty Nation* was a brilliant piece of journalistic Revisionism, and for the time was remarkably accurate. It took some courage in those days." Later, of course, other works, most notably those of Barnes and Sidney B. Fay, superseded Nock's effort. Despite this later work, "Nock's book was an important pioneer work in the history of Revisionism, and one of the best products of any journalist in this field."[13]

Brilliant journalism, however, does not necessarily please book reviewers. Two things, apart from the thesis, irritated reviewers: there was no reference to recently released documents, and the tone tended toward patronization. Both complaints were just. Nock made no pretense about the first, and the second complaint would be heard throughout his career. Nock's tone was always cool, and its disinterestedness often impressed readers as disdain and pretense.

The thesis that Germany was not solely guilty and that Versailles was thus a lie displeased many. Typical of this reaction was a comment in the *New York Times* by Munroe Smith, who seemed to be under the delusion that his statement constituted a refutation: "His version of the diplomatic history of Europe from 1904 to 1914 is substantially that formulated by the German Imperial government during the first months of the war."[14] It could not, therefore, have much validity. A more balanced view was that of O. P. Chitwood, although Mr. Chitwood mistook Nock's avowed distaste for Allied politicians for passion: "To defy successfully a well-intrenched prejudice, a writer should be well-armed with evidence and should be able to present it in a cool, dispassionate manner. The author of this work does not meet either of these tests. The unrestrained partisanship exhibited by him antagonizes the reader and the evidence offered is not sufficient to overcome this antagonism. His range of sources is too narrow."[15] On the contrary, Nock had no more affection for Germany than he did for Britain or France. What he detested was the politician and the diplomat, regardless of nationality.

Only in the rival *New Republic* did Nock find a sympathetic ear in the person of Sidney B. Fay. Fay echoed the demands for more documentation, and wished Nock had seemed less eager to make political capital out of a good position. The book was good, but was journalistic, skimpy, and outdated by little-known, but nevertheless available documents: "We hope Mr. Nock's readable little volume, which originally appeared as articles in the *Freeman*, will have a very wide reading. But we fear his method —and tone—will scarcely convince a majority of those who stand most in need of getting his point of view."[16]

Next to foreign relations, Nock dealt most frequently with the issues of land monopoly, current politics, and the duties of the state. The passion for economic equality in a country of local, small government that had become the core of the Jeffersonian tradition under Henry George and the muckrakers still retained its influence. The hatred of politics and politicians, so evident in Nock's view of diplomacy, was fully as present in his discussion

of domestic affairs. His theory of political action was closely derived from the early Spencer, with only passing mention of in-
definite improvability or survival of the fittest.

Nock stressed the humanizing effects of the proposed land redistribution. Nowhere was it more evident that his concern was
not with money but with the quality of the life. The fact that he
himself was quite poor—indeed, perpetually broke would be
more appropriate—added a certain force to his words, words so
different from those which the liberals and socialists were using.
"I never wished for a change in the economic system for the sake
of a mere redistribution of wealth. That the rich should grow
sheerly poorer and the poor sheerly richer, is nothing to me.
What I want is that everyone should be able to develop the gifts
of the spirit in so far as it is in him to do so." This presupposed
"abundance and leisure for all," but as a means, not an end. Such
things were impossible when deserving men were excluded from
their birthright by exploiting classes. Land monopoly, he emphasized, ruined the exploiter as well as the exploited, "yet the
most casual glance at the personnel of the exploiting class con-
firms it beyond question. Look at them; consider their ways and
occupations, the things that they do and think about!—what can
possibly be said for an economic system that does no better than
that for its very chosen beneficiaries?"[17]

The other important concept to develop in Nock's economics
was the economic interpretation of political science. Nock, a Jeffersonian by instinct, was a democrat by faith. But his particular
definition of "democracy" needed spelling out. This definition
proved important in the subtle shift in emphasis taking place in
Nock's thought at this time—although ideally the people should
rule, in fact they could not. Thus increased suffrage, an important aspect of Jefferson's thought, was less important, and ultimately meaningless. Yet Nock's faith in "democracy" as a civilizing institution was unchanged: "Democracy, in short, is an affair
of economics, not of politics. When one man controls access to
another's source of subsistence, he rules him. . . . No matter what
the form of government may be; no matter whether suffrage be

extended to include children yet unborn; no matter the degree to which the general intelligence is raised; as long as ten per cent keep on owning—owning access to the source of all subsistence, the land, the natural resources—they will rule the ninety per cent; and democracy can not exist."[18]

The state, too, was considered at length. Oppenheimer's book was republished by *Freeman* publisher B. W. Huebsch at this time, and Nock wrote a series of articles on the book and its implications.[19] The first installments of Nock's "The State" were but summations of Oppenheimer's position. Rewritten, these sections later formed some of the introductory parts of Nock's 1935 book, *Our Enemy, The State.* Nock, however, at this earlier date added two ideas to Oppenheimer: the nature of the state was evil (Oppenheimer dealt only with its origin), and Russia was the hope of the world. Like Oppenheimer, Nock hoped and felt that the state, as an antisocial institution, would eventually wither away as men became more suited to the idea of its evil nature.

Because the state was originally a robber, evil by nature, nothing could improve it—not good men, good intentions, nor good circumstances. Much truth could be found, Nock thought, in the despondent observation of John Bright, "that Parliament had done good things, but never . . . simply because it was a good thing." What Bright as well as modern-day liberals and socialists did not see, was that "the state does not act through perversion, but by nature." When it acts in an antisocial way, "it acts as it was meant to act; it acts in accordance with its origin and historical development. When it acts for the common good, it acts against its nature and history."[20] Although fond of referring to himself as an anarchist, Nock, as a result of these views was certainly not a political anarchist in any common sense, even as Spencer was not. When the New York *World* complained that despite the *Freeman* and its faith, "Government will continue on this earth," Nock exclaimed, "As if any person in his right mind ever doubted it!" He then showed what he meant, in a vague way, by "anarchism." "I never saw or heard of an anarchist who did not want his mail carried; who did not want money issued;

who objected to arbitration, either in principle or in practice; who resented the functional activities of a traffic-police or board of public health or board of education. It is only the political and extrafunctional activities of such bodies that he resents."[21] Anarchists such as Benjamin Tucker or Emma Goldman might differ with such a statement, but it does underline one important aspect in any discussion of Nock: he often did not use words the way other people did. He was generally careful to make his meaning clear, but was often misunderstood despite this.

Russia, for Nock as for many intellectuals in the twenties, was the Chance. There, any plan might conceivably have worked out, so thorough seemed the rejection of the Tsarist past. Nock's attitude was a wait-and-see optimism. He saw what could be done; he saw that Russia's diplomats were a cut above most of Europe's; and he saw large natural resources. Russia muffed her chance and betrayed the faith offered to her in the twenties. But her presence then gave a note of optimism to a time when intellectuals were almost universally cynical and pessimistic.

Politics, of course, was always a vicious sham, peopled by Menckenesque boobs eager only for their share of the political means. Good men were rarely found, and when they were they appeared to Nock like ministers in charge of a whore house; no matter how they might attempt reform, they were still running a whore house and there was no way out of it. The good-men-in-office campaign seemed to have produced only pious hypocrites who were also corrupted personally by public office—Woodrow Wilson was the ghost from the past who proved that good men could only do harm in places unsuited to them. One could only withdraw to an Olympus and issue pronouncements on the condition of men, since "great and salutary social transformations, such as in the end do not cost more than they come to, are not effected by political shifts, by movements, by programs and platforms, least of all by violent revolutions, but by sound and disinterested thinking."[22]

Such was the individualism of the mind the *Freeman* emphasized. One might sum up the magazine's views on politics by paraphrasing Friedrich Hayek's comment on Adam Smith: it would be scarcely too much to claim that the main merit of the individualism which they and their friends advocated was that it was a system under which bad men could do the least harm. It was also a system intended to bring out the humanity in any man, unhampered by unnecessary impedimenta.

IV

Of the four men whose writings had deepest influence on Nock, only Matthew Arnold concerned himself with criticism and its theory. Nock looked to him for guidance.

Arnold, as Wimsatt and Brooks have noted, "emerges suddenly . . . the most imposing figure in mid-Victorian criticism, not as a part of the lyric-spasmodic movement, but in a brusque classical resistance to it."[23] One should not, Arnold felt, have too deep an interest in current fads, since the date of a composition mattered little in determining its interest, and from too close a vantage point judgment was difficult: "The Greeks felt, no doubt, with their exquisite sagacity of taste, that an action of present time was too near them, too much mixed up with what was accidental and passing, to form a sufficiently grand, detached, and self-subsistent object for a tragic poem."[24] Evident too in the thoughts of both Nock and Arnold were the ideas of the French religious mystic Joseph Joubert, who believed that the one aim of art in literature was the beautiful. Joubert, in fact, set up criteria which were passed through Arnold to the new humanists and T. S. Eliot: "To accustom mankind to pleasures which depend neither upon the bodily appetites nor upon money, by giving them a taste for the things of the mind, seems to me, in fact, the one proper fruit which nature has meant our literary productions to have."[25] Old and good tended to become synonymous to such a critic, and thus he sometimes mistakenly disparaged the virtues of untried modern forms and ideas. Arnold, like the new humanists later, was deeply concerned with the cultural and political scene of his times, and attempted to use criticism as a social and moral regenerator. Give men a taste of the mind and the universal verities, and they will show less inclination to immorality. As Lionel Trilling has written: "To discover and define, then, the dominant tendency of his age, to analyze the good from the bad, foster the good, diminish the bad —this will be Arnold's program of criticism. Its keynote is activism and affirmation: objectivity, in short."[26] Literature, to such a man, should give an intellectual deliverance from the stultification of the age, and such a deliverance was perfect only "when we have acquired that harmonious acquiescence of mind which we feel in contemplating a grand spectacle that is intelligible to us; when we have lost that impatient irritation of mind which we feel in the presence of an immense, moving, confused spectacle which, while it perpetually excites our curiosity, perpetually baffles our comprehension."[27] Only literature which accomplished this was "adequate." Arnold then believed that true criticism was to be "a disinterested endeavor to learn and propagate the best that is known and thought in the world, and thus establish a current of fresh and true ideas."[28]

Such ideas revealed something about the man, as they revealed something about the men who took them up. As Trilling has remarked, Arnold faced in two directions at once. While welcoming democracy, he knew too well the possible results of it from the French reign of terror; while welcoming a healthy skepticism in religion, he feared the void that the lack of strong religion would cause in men's hearts; he was glad to see the old perish, yet he feared that much good would perish too; he wished for progress, yet feared for the values which expansion would bring. Thus he found himself both supporting and attacking the old, and welcoming yet qualifying the new. His criticism was, "in effect, his refusal to move forward until Burke and Voltaire compounded their quarrel, bowed to each other and, taking him by either hand, agreed on the path to follow."[29] Such a statement would be equally true if said of Nock, who relished the old and wished for an economic utopia.

In his own work, Nock first made the important distinction

between a reviewer and a critic. A reviewer was one who notices and summarizes what was new—"a kind of glorified and disinterested advertising." Because he enjoyed such work, Nock did a good deal of it after he retired from active literary life (1939–45), but very little during the *Freeman* years.

A critic, on the other hand, concerned himself only with the best, whether it was old or new. Unless a work has a true place in the long course of good work, the critic rightfully has nothing to do with it. Certainly he never wastes his time writing about it. An ordinary man was permitted to ask only three things of a critic: "First, tell me what you like, because ten to one it is what I too, like. . . . Second, tell me why you like it, because then I can justify to myself my own taste, and it is always pleasant to be able to do that since 'all mankind naturally desireth knowledge'. . . . Third, tell me where what you like is to be found, because I do not want to waste my time and energy."[30]

The best way to illustrate this guide was to use it on a particular work. Among those Nock chose was one of Gogol's stories from "Evenings at a Dikanka Farmhouse." "Le but essentiel de l'art," he wrote, quoting a favorite sentiment, "est d'élever l'homme audessus de la vie vulgaire, et de réveiller en lui le sentiment de son origine céleste,"[31] a sentiment which could be absorbed into the Jeffersonian tradition without difficulty. Nock, during this time, retained his faith in the essential good taste of the mass man (even while becoming disillusioned with his political performance) if only he could be freed from the pernicious influence of bad literature. This optimism soon disappeared.

Returning to Gogol, Nock postulated the need for a "*temper*, a frame of mind," which would give the critic a correct insight. This temper had three aspects: disinterestedness, "the temper which *floats* that method and makes it free to do its best," and enabled one to deal with great emotions and great spiritual experiences; a "profound and genuine tenderness" for the characters portrayed; and a serenity which enabled one to disregard passing eruptions and concentrate on the best aspects of life. As Arnold wrote of Wordsworth,

The cloud of human destiny,
Others will front it fearlessly
But who, like him, will *put it by?*[32]

Thus one obtained the method of criticism and the greater philosophical view which gave it its place in life. Good literature, like the Gogol story, in pointing out the good and evil in life through study of the proper temper of the best in humanity, was important in the good life. It was, properly, one of the most important aspects of an education. The critic, however, had an intermediary goal: he had to show modern writers where past faults lay, and how they could be avoided in the production of future works. This position bore an outward resemblance to the new humanist criticism—both were developments of Arnold's thought—but Nock was at pains to show that, in their own way, the professors could be as stifling of good standards and work as they claimed Mencken and the naturalists to be. "The work, say, of Mr. More, Mr. Babbitt, Mr. Brownell, Mr. Sherman—taking a few names more or less at random—seems chiefly concerned with establishing a position and fortifying itself in that position." Such activity was a part of criticism, and not to be disparaged, but everyone did it, and so great critics did not need to bother themselves over it. Criticism had other business: "Its business is to help the artist, the writer; not only by providing him with examples of great art and by competently analysing and expounding these examples, but more, far more, by *prepossessing* him, by interesting him in classic work, by awakening his feeling for it and helping him to see for himself how lovely and delightful it is, and to anticipate the satisfaction that comes from a sincere and enthusiastic effort to emulate it." Arnold, he concluded, not only told one what to do, he managed to infect one with "a pestering desire to do it." This was "the acme of critical method."[33]

V

Nock viewed literature and religion as equally necessary and complementary in the pursuit of the good life. Religion was firmly in the Hellenistic camp of the beloved Arnold. He had little sympathy for the Hebraist, who put so much emphasis on orthodoxy and dogma that he lost the temper of the religious life. For, like the best in literature, religion was "a *temper,* a frame of mind; the fruit of the Spirit is, as St. Paul says, love, joy, peace, long-suffering, gentleness, goodness, faith, meekness, self-control."[34]

During the *Freeman* years, fundamentalists and modernists sparred sporadically about the importance of such dogmatic tenets as the virgin birth and the resurrection. The *New Republic* and the *Nation* tended toward support of the modernist camp, while the Catholic *America* and the fundamentalist journals supported the other camp. Nock refused to take sides. The arguments, he said quietly, dealt not with the truths of religion but with truths of science, and that therefore the religious man need have nothing to do with them. Such arguments "may be, and very often are, put to a religious use . . . but they are not in themselves matters of religion." They were interesting, but the interest was scientific, not religious. "Religion is the highest effort of the human spirit toward perfection; it is an enthusiastic inward motion towards what St. Paul called 'the fruits of the spirit.'" One needed only remark that the doctrine of the virgin birth bore little relevance to progress toward the fruits of the spirit, and the argument was shown to be nugatory.[35]

Nock's own interpretation of Scripture was explicit. His career in the ministry was the ideal exposure to theology, while his later secular career enabled him to reflect out loud without fear of censure from Hebraist fellow clergy. "The history of organized Christianity is the most depressing study I ever undertook, and also one of the most interesting,"[36] he wrote, for the organized church, like the state, was of value to the individual only as a cross to bear, and performed proper functions in inverse proportion to the number of its members. The institutional church, furthermore, could not be blamed on its nominal founder: "By all that is known of Jesus, He appears to have been as sound and simon-pure an individualist as Lao-Tze. His teaching seems to have been purely individualistic in its intent. One would say He had no idea whatever of its being formulated into an institutional charter, or a doctrinal hurdle to be got over by those desirous of being called by His Name."[37] No proof exists that Jesus ever formulated any doctrines other than those of a universal loving God and the universal brotherhood of man. His life was led to show men how such a life as He proposed might be led. He remarked that if all men would lead such lives, there would be established a Kingdom of Heaven on earth, an expression which He did not further define. In a word, He meant: "If every *one* would reform *one* (that is to say, oneself) and keep *one* steadfastly following the way of life which He recommended, the Kingdom of Heaven would be coextensive with human society. The teaching of Jesus, simple as it was, was brand-new to those who listened to it. Conduct, 'morality touched by emotion,' put forth as the whole sum of religion, was something they had never heard of."[38] Thus Jesus had set up a difficult counsel of perfection for men to try for. Many would be unable to make it, but this did not excuse them from the attempt. Evidence showed that during the first dozen decades or so, Christians followed such devices. Later, the same forces that corrupted society through the state caused Christianity to become the stepchild of a state, and under such conditions, religious faith was no longer the only motive for membership. The growth of the church from the period no later than the fourth century A.D. had been away from the teachings of Jesus. Thus the true Christian joined a church in spite of its dogma, ritual, and banality of thought.

VI

Placing Nock in the context of intelligent thought in the early twentieth century is not easy. Morton White, in his study of the path-breakers Dewey, Holmes, Beard, Veblen, and so on, has labeled the movement "the revolt against formalism." These men, White feels, turned toward "historicism," the attempt to explain facts by reference to earlier facts, and "cultural organi-cism," or the use of social sciences other than the one specifically under investigation to find answers and explanations. The his-toricist looks to what happened in the past, the organicist to what is happening in the present. Opposing these men were those of the old school, the formalists, who were devoted to ab-stract reasoning and who preferred logic to experience, the ideal to the actual. This system of classification is valid for the men White treats, but is not especially helpful in speaking of Nock. Nock was originally willing to experiment, like Dewey; he had views about businessmen similar to Veblen's; he was too much of an individualist not to appreciate the humanity of Holmes' approach to law; and he borrowed wholesale from, and heartily endorsed, Beard's work in American history. Yet he op-posed these men on almost every political question that arose after the war, and was particularly scornful of much of Dewey's work on education.

More useful instruments of classification would be the terms "inductive" and "deductive" reasoning. The deductive reasoner would, like Plato, Spencer, or Hegel, postulate certain given presuppositions, and work out a philosophy from these deduc-tively, from principle to phenomena. The other group, which would include White's antiformalists and the British empiricists, would observe first the phenomena and then induce universal principles from these phenomena. Using this scheme, Nock would be firmly in the camp of the deductive reasoners. His normal method of operation was to take a principle, such as Ar-nold's concept of culture or Spencer's concept of happiness, and apply it to whatever might arise. The fact that he might borrow some principle established by a member of the inductive camp matters not at all. The division is purely one of method, and says nothing about the material that is used. Thus when Beard went to the facts and derived from them the terms "personality" and "reality" in his first book, establishing the principle of class in-terest in political theory, Nock could use this principle as a fact in his *Jefferson* without changing his basic approach.

The unfortunate aspect of this type of thought is that when the principle used is based on a fallacy, as the single tax was based on the fallacy of human perfectibility, the arguments deduced from the principle are invalid and even harmful. In the thirties, Nock had second thoughts about some of his presuppositions, and changed them. In the twenties, however, certain books containing these principles had entirely too much influence on him and weakened his work. "Substitute Bibles, giving religious comfort," Lewis Mumford has called the books Nock mistakenly relied on.

Yet even while this tendency existed Nock was improving, becoming more and more an authority and less and less a cultured dabbler. Considering the innocence of the *American Magazine* years, when Rabelais, Arnold, and the ancients were his guides and the Golden Rule as preached by Lincoln Steffens the *sine qua non* of progressive protest, the remarkable thing was how far Nock had developed. Even Francis Neilson, in his reminiscences of the *Freeman*, remarked on Nock's development, although as usual his catty jealousy is offensive: "Those who came across Nock during the thirties and fell under his sway met an entirely different person. That Nock I did not know, and that one did not exist in the days of *The Freeman*. Some of my friends could not make out what had happened to bring about a change so remarkable."[39] Nock, in perpetual bad health and with his eccentric mannerisms, was incomprehensible to Neilson, who later accused him of a variety of sins, ranging from bad posture and timidity in taking a stand (!) to sciolism (on the ground that Nock did not like to argue or converse in the languages he quoted in writing). Much of this animosity stemmed from temperament, and the bitterness came only later, at what Neilson regarded as outright dishonesty. Neilson was, in fact, wrong in his assumptions, as unpublished letters show, but the quarrel is unimportant here.[40]

A certain antipathy between Nock and Neilson apparently existed in the *Freeman* office during much of its existence. As Lewis Mumford has said, "Nock couldn't bear Neilson's somewhat inflated parliamentary style; and he would quietly put Neilson's contributions in the drawer of his desk, letting them gather dust there, publishing as few as possible. It says something for the character of both men that they kept together as long as the *Freeman* actually did last."[41] Nock was ill; the *Freeman* was running a deficit of upwards of $80,000 yearly; and most important, the readership never went beyond the 7,000 range, thus giving the editors the disconcerting feeling of laboring in a vacuum. And so the *Freeman* closed.

Oswald Garrison Villard, still with the *Nation,* wrote the eulogy of the *Freeman.* Despite the scars of past quarrels, Villard expressed his "profound regret" at the demise of "the best written and most brilliantly edited of the weeklies of protest." He went on:

> It is true that the *Freeman* has been limited by belief in a panacea, the freeing of the land. It is also true that it has not been willing to advocate reforms of a palliative character; it did not feel it its duty to make practical suggestions of immediate value. So it had to encounter much conventional fault-finding, as if criticism—self-criticism—were not the primary need of the hour in America. The memory of its vigorous differences from *The Nation* does not prevent us from expressing our sorrow that the *Freeman* is to go, our grateful thanks that it has existed, and our belief that it would be a misfortune if some other medium were not found to avail itself of Mr. Albert Jay Nock's exceptional equipment for editorial service.[42]

Shortly after the appearance of this editorial, Nock sailed for Europe, as he seemed to do after every major event in his life.

*JOURNEYMAN SCHOLAR, 1924-39

This is not the last crisis in human affairs. The world will go on somehow, and more crises will follow. It will go on best, however, if among us there are more who have stood apart, who refused to be anxious or too much concerned, who were cool and enquiring and had their eyes on a longer past and a longer future.

By their example they can remind us that the passing moment is only a moment; by their loyalty they will have cherished those things which only the disinterested mind can use.

—WALTER LIPPMANN

CHAPTER SEVEN

BIOGRAPHER:

Artemus Ward, Thomas Jefferson, Francis Rabelais, Henry George

THE last issue of the *Freeman* was dated March 5, 1924. Nock, on his way to Brussels, was distinguished as a wit, an editor, and a radical. His only book was a reprint of journalistic forays into history. For the next fifteen years, he consolidated this reputation and made a new one as one of the most distinguished essayists in America. His iconoclasm, endearing to some and annoying to others, gave a unique quality to his writings. Because of the superb quality of his prose style, his essays achieved a permanent place in the history of American letters. He had come a long way from the obscure clergyman recently added to the staff of the *American Magazine*, of whom John Reed could write,

> To point a tale, to drive dull care away,
> NOCKO then reads a bit of Rabelais.
> So time passes, sped with royal fun
> Till the white tower booms the stroke of One.[1]

The next fifteen years, through the publication of *Henry George* in 1939, might be called the "journeyman scholar" years. Nock took constant trips abroad, to Belgium, Luxembourg, Portugal, and France. He contributed regularly to most of the leading magazines, from *Harper's* and the *Atlantic* to the *Virginia Quarterly Review*. He wrote three biographical studies which are among the most lasting examples of his work. Finally, he had two mildly taxing jobs, first as editorial assistant on Suzanne La Follette's *New Freeman* and later on Paul Palmer's *American Mercury*, and second as visiting professor of politics and American history at the Bard College branch of Columbia (1931–33).

There was nothing surprising about the editorial posts. Nock enjoyed magazine work, and as contributor and consultant he could enjoy the pleasures without the onerous burdens that had taken up his time with the *Freeman*. The visiting professorship, however, was another matter, and many of Nock's friends were hard put to decide how his good friend, Bernard Iddings Bell, had been able to persuade him to take it. As Ellery Sedgwick saw it, Armageddon was close at hand:

> My Dear Nock:
> There's a new heaven and a new earth. I open the simplest of communications from Warden Bell, and find the news that you are a professor. You, the Ambassador of Heathendom, are accredited to a most Christian college. Verily, wonder is not departed from this world. Bell has the blessed characteristic of originality. He must have thought of this thing; not you—for though you think no man's thoughts, your imagination never flew so far as this.
> You can see the thought stirs me. What fun those young men will have chasing the tails of your ideas. Jefferson, du Bellay, Gargantua, Artemus Ward—what a Squad in Heaven looks down upon you with their blessing.
> As for me, I am so glad you will be kept in this country. Every outrage that it offers your susceptibilities will sandpaper your soul.
> Yours sincerely,
> E.S.[2]

Nock, however, was soon fed up with the unintelligent masses who took up space in his classroom, and his stay at Bard was brief. His reasons for leaving will be obvious when I examine his essays on education.

Nock's writing during these fifteen years can best be divided into three areas: articles and books on Artemus Ward, Jefferson, Rabelais, and Henry George; the essays on the "quality of civilization in the United States," explicitly on the nature of the civilized life, women and morals, and education; and the political essays, dealing with the means of attaining the civilized life.

Certain new patterns emerged in his writing during this period. His faith in the single tax, so dominant from 1910 until well into the *Freeman* years, declined. His appreciation of Henry George as a philosopher never waned, but he detested George's use of the philosophy as a political campaign platform. Nock never explicitly renounced the single tax, he simply stopped mentioning it. His loss of faith in perfectible men made practical belief in George's cure for society impossible, but nothing interfered with his appreciation of George's analysis of the problem. Jefferson remained the touchstone, and Nock constantly referred to his ideal man for precedent; but, increasingly, the Jefferson who had served so well as a liberal and a radical became a conservative Jefferson. This is not an unlikely development when a radical tradition has become accepted over a long period of time. An old revolution can, by prescription, become conservative orthodoxy. Jefferson himself had become more and more conservative, especially in his correspondence with Adams, and Nock looked on this correspondence as one of the greatest episodes in the man's life.

The major change which made the period noteworthy in Nock's career was his adoption of an élitist social theory within his Jeffersonian framework. Jefferson, and later Matthew Arnold, had prepared Nock for such a position. The essential characteristic was Arnold's idea of *humanity* as the ultimate good to be cultivated in an individual. Nock's development of this theme was a major contribution to American political thought in the 1930's.

II

Nock had explicit views on the subject of biography. With his strong feelings of personal integrity and privacy, he had a marked distaste for the debunking, profane, sexually gymnastic works that passed under his eyes during the twenties and thirties. Biography, including autobiography, should have but one purpose, "to help the historian." Anything else was but a nugatory attempt to raise sales and encourage the ignorant to feel that they had learned something significant: "I suspect that the popular appetite for 'readable' biography is symptomatic not only of a low and prurient curiosity, but also, when this motive is not dominant, of a wish to live exclusively on predigested cultural food, which no one can do. A passive and workless *Ersatz*-knowledge of illustrious men seems to me to reflect our national ideals of a passive and workless *Ersatz*-education, a passive and workless *Ersatz*-culture; ideals which we are beginning to see are illusory."[3] Nock approached his subjects in this spirit.

> A nation is a soul, a spiritual principle evoked by the common possession of a rich legacy of remembrances, and by the will to keep improving this hereditary property for the benefit of those who shall receive it hereafter in their turn. "Man does not improvise himself," said Renan, austerely; a nation, like an individual, is the culmination of an age-long spiritual tendency; and therefore the cult of ancestors is the soundest of all cults, because it is our ancestors who have made us what we are.[4]

The quotation had reference not to Jefferson but to Artemus Ward, the writer who was born in 1834, and whose thirty-three years were spent in commenting on the American scene. Ward, whose real name was Charles Farrar Browne, earned his reputation primarily as a humorist. For this quality he was most often remembered. But the soul of a nation had little real need for a long-dead humorist, and Nock felt that Ward deserved mention for other reasons.

At the time Nock wrote, the British could obtain a complete Ward at any bookstore. The *Times Literary Supplement* of April 26, 1934, gave him the entire front page and a runover onto the second. Yet in Ward's own country, not one paper observed this, the hundredth anniversary of his birth. Nock hoped, in his three essays on Ward,[5] to make up for this neglect.

"I suggest," he wrote, "that Ward was the first really great critic of American society, and that in this capacity he remains today, as he said of his Grate show, 'ekalled by few and exceld by none.' "[6] Nock believed that what Aristotle called the "determination of the judicious" established the validity of criticism. Ward, he felt, gave a remarkably complete appraisal of the "American psychology." Furthermore, he did not encumber his views with himself. "There are very few aspects of our collective life which he does not illuminate and exhibit as they really are, rather than as distorted by the myopia of prepossession or the delirium of vanity." Like a good artist, he accomplished this indirectly, and so powerfully impressed the reader "with an attitude of mind, a mood, a temper"—the criteria Nock had taken from Arnold for his *Freeman* criticism.[7]

Ward the critic lived in a society similar in cant, hypocrisy, and charlatanry to the America of the twenties and thirties, and because he never "encumbered truth with himself," his writings were more lasting than those of others who wrote of the same events. He appealed to that disorganized group of people capable of appreciating incisive critical perception: those who have *Intelligenz*, which Nock defined as the power "to see things as they are, to survey them and one's own relations to them with objective disinterestedness, and to apply one's consciousness to them simply and directly, letting it take its own way over them uncharted by prepossession, unchanneled by prejudice, and above all uncontrolled by routine and formula."[8]

On top of this, Ward the critic also had the saving element of humanity which Nock so cherished. He felt, Nock thought, that life must be felt as a joy, and that through such a bond "the called and chosen spirits" kept together. Ward did not moralize or attempt reform, he concerned himself only with the "joyful appraisal, assessment, and representation" of life as he saw it.[9] Nock found similar qualities in other literary criticism he wrote.

Apparently, he became an élitist in art years before he became one in politics.

III

During the *Freeman* years, Nock asked several of the younger men associated with the magazine to do a work on Jefferson, showing the man's true qualities. Most works on Jefferson available at the time concentrated on politics, the Declaration of Independence, or other public aspects of the man's life. Nock viewed Jefferson as a private personality far more valuable than these works imagined. No one, however, fulfilled his request, and when he went to Brussels after the closing of the *Freeman*, he decided to do the work himself. For two years, usually in Brussels, he worked on his study. It was published in 1926.

The preference for working on men's minds rather than on the institutions that affect them was an obvious factor in Nock's work on the *Freeman*. It appeared again in *Jefferson*. "You will have the satisfaction of seeing this book work in just the way the *Freeman* worked," he wrote to a friend, "—quietly and persistently undermining the strongholds of superstition." His book would work exactly as the *Freeman* had, in the minds of men, "very quietly and for a long time, and with an effect entirely disproportionate to the amount of fuss made over it."[10]

The centennial year of Jefferson's death was 1926, and Nock's book was at first overshadowed by Claude Bowers' impressive and well-received *Jefferson and Hamilton*. Nock's book made good his prophecy. It was the first book to make an extended case for the "cultural" as opposed to the "political" or "mythical" Jefferson, and influenced much of the scholarship that succeeded it.[11] Thirty-five years afterwards, Merrill Peterson awarded the prize to Nock over Bowers and the others who had since written on Jefferson. Nock's book, although less noticed, he wrote, was "able to work its way in the quieter corridors of the mind." In retrospect, it was the more enduring book and is now "the most captivating single volume in the Jefferson literature."[12]

The book made no pretense to being a biography. Nock saw no sense in merely pointing out items that were available elsewhere. The book was "a mere study—a study in conduct and character,"[13] and as such it took many liberties with normal historical tenets of importance. It was basically a study of the workings of Jefferson's mind, infinitely more important to Nock than the particular offices Jefferson might have held. Thus the descriptions of Jefferson's architectural, botanical, and linguistic interests took up more room than the politics of the independence period. One knew, after reading the book, more about Jefferson's ability as a surveyor than one did about his leadership of the Republicans.

The other distinctive feature of the book was the almost total reliance on Beard's work for factual data and on Oppenheimer and Henry George for theoretical analysis. To Nock, the politics of Jefferson, Hamilton, or any other of the founding fathers were explicable only in terms of class interests. Jefferson in this respect was "but little more than a theoretical democrat than Hamilton. To view him as a theoretical or doctrinaire democrat is to disregard the most inadmissible inconsistencies, both in his public acts and in his expressions of governmental theory—inconsistencies which resolve themselves immediately when one views him as the representative of an economic class interest."[14]

With the exception of those who objected to the economic emphases, reviewers were generally either favorable or ecstatic. Stuart Sherman thought Nock's Jefferson was "a character with a strong spiritual likeness to Marcus Aurelius as depicted by Matthew Arnold,"[15] and praised the book highly. Samuel Eliot Morison found a number of historical errors that he disliked, yet he praised the "brilliancy" of the book.[16] Claude Bowers thought the book a gem, and his opinion was widely echoed. Bowers acclaimed the "charm of a lucid style," without "any straining after an epigram." The book was "charming in style, penetrating in interpretation, and written without prejudice," and he congratulated Nock "upon a fine literary achievement."[17]

The Mr. Jefferson Nock painted—the name was always

chastely prefaced by the "Mr."—was, unsurprisingly, similar to his creator. He was a "libertarian practitioner of taste and manners" to "whom conduct was three fourths of life and good taste nine tenths of conduct." Jefferson was "a distinguished man, an excellent man—a great man, if you like—but the fact remained that he had always been persistently on the side of some wholly impossible loyalty." One could see how such a man might appeal to the editor of the *Freeman*, expounding the truths of the single tax in a virtual vacuum, in a world where mass culture was a contradiction in terms. Jefferson was to Nock the unique individual in a democratic society, a kind of divine contradiction; he was successful in public life without sacrificing honor, character, or virtue, a politician who would rather lose than pimp second-rate ideas for the masses. Further, he seemed to have an ingrained predilection toward Nock's favorite eccentricity: "*Hide thy life*, said Epicurus; and no one ever succeeded better than Thomas Jefferson at hiding his inner springs of sentiment. He was the most approachable and the most impenetrable of men, easy and delightful of acquaintance, impossible of knowledge."[18]

As might be expected, Nock saw Jefferson the man as not contradicting the Jeffersonian tradition. Unlike Professor Gilbert Chinard, who painted Jefferson as the "Apostle of Americanism," Nock thought that Jefferson was what Americanism should have been modeled after, but was not. Rather, a specious Americanism had grown up in his name.

Jefferson was not particularly concerned about the land problem because of the unlimited abundance of America, but when he saw poverty in France he came to a conclusion not incompatible with the single tax. Wherever there is in any country uncultivated land, Jefferson thought, the unemployed poor have been victimized by violation of their natural rights. The earth was "given as a common stock for man to labour and live on,"[19] precisely the doctrine Nock had emphasized in his *American Magazine* tax articles.

But Jefferson was more than a sound land philosopher or theorizer on natural rights. He was a man of culture, and knew that freedom was necessary for the full flowering of character. Neither Jefferson nor Nock thought that real happiness could exist without freedom. The majority was owned by the masters, and the masters were slaves to their vices, and so no one was happy, no one could achieve humanity. Man needed economic and social equality, since "even the sense of taste and manners, so admirable, so interesting and prepossessing, is superficial and ineffectual in the absence of liberty. . . ."[20]

Rural America looked better than ever. Cities seemed inherently evil, and a powerful government nothing but a tormentor. But Jefferson was never really tempted. He was only storing up recommendations for the environment that was blessedly free of the diseases of Europe. Given land and freedom, what then? Keep power local, since "a single consolidated government would become the most corrupt government on earth." These words had added force for Nock in the thirties. Had not his *homme idéal* exclaimed: "What an augmentation of the field for jobbing, speculating, plundering, office-building and office-hunting would be produced by an assumption of all the State powers into the hands of the General Government!"[21]

Jefferson was particularly enamored of the division of the country into wards, and could always be found in support of the smallest unit possible, whether it be state, city, ward, or, most of all, the person. But danger was ever present, for what sort of men would be drawn to politics? Even the hallowed Washington had had trouble filling his second cabinet. Like Nock, Jefferson felt that rottenness of conduct and a desire for public office went hand in hand, and thus "the natural progress of things is for liberty to yield and government to gain ground."[22] With these views, Nock saw Jefferson as a working miracle. Even Jefferson's vitriolic enemy John Randolph acknowledged this, for Jefferson "was the only man I knew or ever heard of, who really, truly, and honestly, not only said *Nolo episcopari*, but actually refused the mitre."[23]

Although not a pacifist, Jefferson did not want war because of the weakness of the fledgling nation and because nothing could be gained from such a policy. He had, however, no overwhelming affection for either France or England, despite federalist charges of Francophilia: "As for France and England," Jefferson wrote to John Adams, "with all their progress in science, the one is a den of robbers, and the other of pirates."[24] It was not that he loved the French more, but that he disliked them less: "Of all nations on earth, the British require to be treated with the most *hauteur*. They require to be kicked into common good manners."[25] As a witty saying of the time had it, "there was no such thing as good manners in England, but only the right and wrong kind of bad manners."[26] To a cultivated practitioner of taste and manners like Jefferson, such things were important.

In economics Jefferson was sadly deficient in knowledge, but with many of the right instincts. "He was a natural free trader,"[27] but despite this, he accepted the principle of retaliatory tariffs, and with the Embargo Act "proposed a measure wholly subversive of the principle of liberty and fraught with far more serious economic consequences and with political consequences at least as serious."[28] He held out against Hamilton on taxation and the national bank for the wrong reasons, and his failure to understand his errors "may be said to have made his own fiscal measures almost as bad for the producer, in the long run, as Hamilton's."[29] But to Jefferson as a gentleman, argument of this sort with Hamilton was displeasing, and Jefferson always lost these battles. "He was a poor disputant; contention of any kind was distasteful to him, as having at best a touch of vulgarity about it."[30]

Jefferson also appeared in Nock's book as an élitist, and the mention of this point also distinguished Nock's book from those which portrayed Jefferson as an undiscriminating democrat. The point was important, for in the years in which *Jefferson* was being written, Nock's own élitism was growing stronger, and was implied in his writings of the twenties, even though he did not make his specific statement of it until almost ten years later. Jefferson overestimated the value of literacy in forming an intelligent public, but he was never a leveler. His notion of the limitation of education at public expense was "as explicit as his notion of limited suffrage," which he propounded at about the same time. He was well aware that it was possible "for a man's education to be too much for his abilities." He wished each ward to have a school, "open to all for instruction in reading, writing, and common arithmetic." Nock was at pains to point out Jefferson's brutality in not burdening the public with the education of anyone but the most talented. The boy of best genius was picked out of the primary school and sent to grammar school. All but the very best at grammar school would be dismissed after a year or two. The leading scholar would continue for six years. Perhaps twenty would finally remain, the best half of which would go to William and Mary, and the rest would be turned adrift. Children paying their own way could go to any school they pleased, for Jefferson dealt only with state obligation.[31] Jefferson's view was adopted in France, and is still the guide there. The American system of education was never Jefferson's. Those who used his name were either unable to read or charlatans, if they thought he had been a supporter of subsidized education for all past the primary years.

Jefferson also appeared to be regrettably backward about the role of women, consigning them to domestic duties and ignorance. He did, however, have an exemplary hatred of newspapers, and knew that the spirit of rebellion against the state was one of the most valuable assets a people could retain. Further, Jefferson had a kind of mystic faith without the encumbrances of Hebraic religious practices. "The moral and religious nature of man," Nock wrote, "presents many attractive problems to the metaphysician, but Mr. Jefferson had a pretty clear conviction, in the first place, that these problems are insoluble and, moreover, that their solution, even if one might attain it, would have so little bearing on the practical conduct of life that speculation about them had best be left to those who have nothing better to do."[32] Jefferson was a deist; he believed that God existed, although His existence was not subject to the usual canons of proof. Hence contentions about the matter were of no value.

This, then, was Nock's Jefferson—deficient in economics, disliking any arguments, content to lead one life well. Jefferson was the man who had found the quality of joy in life, the man who could not be denied a place in Arnold's humanity. He was the man of quality who possessed "a dominant sense of form and order, a commanding instinct for measure, harmony, and balance, unfailingly maintained for four-score years toward the primary facts of human life—toward discipline and training, toward love, parenthood, domesticity, art, science, religion, friendship, business, social and communal relations. . . ."[33] This was Jefferson the man who could not be anything but a sublime accident in a political democracy.

IV

Jefferson may have been the ideal man, but Rabelais was the ideal spirit, who provided the gaiety and joy that Nock desired. "Rabelais was one of the world's great libertarians," he wrote to Mrs. Evans, "and if I can do anything for him with American readers of the more thoughtful kind, I shall be truly happy; he has been a stay and support to my spirit for thirty years, and I could not possibly have got through without him. . . ."[34] Nock's essay on Rabelais was a work of sheer devotion, a cheerful attempt to repay a debt that could never really be repaid.

"Spirit" was the key word to Nock's Dr. Rabelais, and he left no possibility of doubt about where his appreciation of Rabelais originated.

It must be laid down once and for all, that the chief purpose of reading a classic like Rabelais is to prop and stay the spirit, especially in its moments of weakness and enervation, against the stress of life, to elevate it above the reach of commonplace annoyances and degradations, and to purge it of despondency and cynicism. . . . The current aspect of our planet, and the performances upon it, are not always encouraging, and one therefore turns with unspeakable gratitude to those who themselves have been able to contemplate them with equanimity and are able to help others to do so. In their writings one sees how the main preoccupations, ambitions, and interests of mankind appear when regarded "in the view of eternity," and one is insensibly led to make that view one's own. Thus Rabelais is one of the half-dozen writers whose spirit in a conscious way pervades and refreshes one's being, tempers, steadies, and sweetens it, so that one lays the book aside conscious of a new will to live up to the best of one's capacity. . . .[35]

Miss Catherine Rose Wilson, Nock's Vassar- and Oxford-educated collaborator, did most of his research, while Nock did the synthesizing and writing. The two began work shortly after Nock completed *Jefferson. Francis Rabelais, The Man and his Work* was first published in 1929, and then, two years later, as the introduction to an edition of the complete, annotated translation of Rabelais by Urquhart and Motteux. The reviews were generally favorable, with one notable exception. Eliseo Vivas, in the *Nation*, took exception both to Nock's spirit and method. He felt that Nock and Miss Wilson lacked the necessary qualifications for Rabelais criticism. They had, he felt, two fundamental defects. They approached their subject "in a spirit of unmixed piety," and they tried to "demonstrate too simple a thesis." Vivas felt that they had made Rabelais "a breviary for the comfort of those whose weariness and squeamish disgust with the conditions of our day impel toward consolation." Life in Rabelais's time, he said, was no more enlightened than life in the present day. But Rabelais did not seek comfort in the past, he lived "with a dash and a relish incomprehensible to us." He laughed at the imbecilities of his time, "but he derived no small measure of enjoyment from it. This is the true Pantagruelism."[36] Vivas had a point, although no two people agreed exactly on the best way to approach a great writer. The trouble with this criticism was that it tended to make Rabelais nothing more or less than a Mencken who wrote fiction instead of essays. Nock and Miss Wilson both had enormous respect for Rabelais, but piety was not part of it; deep and permanent appreciation perhaps would be more accurate. Who could say definitely that this approach was not the most effective?

Most reviewers were favorable, and echoed Ben Ray Redman's praise in the *Herald-Tribune*: "It is the book, the one book,
so far as I know, for any reader who requires help toward a clear,
clean, unobstructed view of the temper of one of the world's
great writers."[37] "Temper" of course was the key word, and
Nock, had he read the review, would have appreciated the term.

Nock's Rabelais was first of all a humanist, of the tradition in
which Arnold, Jeremy Taylor, and other Nock favorites found a
place. Humanism, Nock wrote, "is selfless, consistent, invariable
and the same for all mankind." It was distinterested and objective and it contained the other qualities Nock felt necessary in a
critic. Like all of Nock's ventures into biography, *Francis Rabelais* was dominated by these criteria. Nock used them himself;
he found them in the topics he discussed—indeed, he chose the
topics because of this quality. All Nock biographies were alike
in this way. His style did not develop from biography to biography, nor were the changes in his own views reflected in his
works on others. One cannot date a book of Nock's on somebody
else by the commentary of the author, so consistent was the point
of view. Humanism, to such a writer, was another name for the
view of the true critic.[38]

The humanist believed in an orderly, meaningful nature—the
keystone of nineteenth century liberalism. He disliked the me-
dieval world of theology and philosophy, and the "empty noth-
ings" that were considered problems by theologians. He was, in
fact, "invincibly suspicious" of any philosophical formulation
which got too far from the practical and the necessary. But the
guiding force of humanism to Nock was what he called "Pantagruelism," the spirit of Pantagruel. This spirit Nock called "superiority," for Pantagruel never let himself be vexed or dismayed
by anything. He regarded the world with a serene and occasionally bawdy good humor, unshakably above all the petty cares
of the rest of the world. Nock's view of history as inevitable and
his good-humored fatalism stemmed from this analysis of Rabelaisian spirits. The mundane simply was not important, and that
was all a man of learning could say about it.[39]

The humanist did not believe in reformers, and Nock pointed out Rabelais's portrait of Homenas as an example of what Mencken called the "uplifter" or "wowser." Homenas was the great inquisitor who called for "uninterrupted eternal peace through the universe, an end to all wars, plunderings, drudgeries, robbing, assassinates (unless it be to destroy those cursed rebels, the heretics)"—the eternal moralist, making the world safe for orthodoxy. Everyone will be happy, provided he be no heretic. One has a distinct impression that Wilson's Fourteen Points, along with censorship of any kind and attempts at forced reformation are all lineal descendants of Homenas's "eternal decretals" to Nock.[40]

In Rabelais, too, Nock found the spirit of hedonism which he called his own. Like anarchism, hedonism to Nock meant something different from what it meant to others. The term referred to Pantagruelism, and was not concerned with either pleasure of sensuality, but with joy. It connected individualism, freedom, noninterference in the affairs of others, and the ever-present superiority to the demands of the mundane life.

Nock outlined this philosophy in a speech at Johns Hopkins University on October 28, 1932, at a celebration of the four-hundredth anniversary of the publication of *Pantagruel*. In this speech was the typical combination that reoccurred in many of his writings: an undertone of seriousness constantly kept alive by easy wit and a deep insight that never seemed tragic, despite the pessimism of almost all his predictions. "Pantagruelism is not a cult or a creed or a frame of mind," he said, "but a quality of spirit. In one place Rabelais says it is 'a certain jollity of mind pickled in the scorn of fortune,' and this is one of its aspects: an easy, objective, genial, but unyielding superiority to everything external, to every conceivable circumstance of one's life."

But Pantagruelism was more than a quality of spirit. Its essence was that of individualism: "Pantagruelism means keeping the integrity of one's own personality absolutely intact." It was, furthermore, "utterly unselfconscious; it works like a kind of secondary instinct."[41] In this area, the reasons for Nock's antipathy to American life were more apparent, as were the reasons, in fact, that he spent much of the last twenty years of his life in Brussels. To him, the American had sacrificed himself to his business and made a religion out of work. "Puritanism is always being blamed for the wrong thing. Its various taboos never did half as much real harm to the spirit of mankind as its doctrine of a divine sanction for work."[42] The Pantagruelist could not operate this way. The true Pantagruelist "never admits that there is anything in the world that is bigger than he is." Business, status, or public approval mean nothing to him. For example, Nock continued, an analysis of American business would show just how far it had gone from the Pantagruelian ideal. The typical American businessman had allowed business to get bigger than he was, in the name of progress, civilization, and social esteem. Americans had sought greatness by subordinating themselves to an institution they thought great, so they might have greatness reflected on them. Such people, Nock remarked, are "like the misguided girl who had lived with so many gentlemen that she thought she was a lady. . . ."[43]

Even though his mind knew better, Nock's spirit was captivated by this Rabelaisian ideal of Pantagruelism. Van Wyck Brooks, like Hendrik Willem Van Loon and others, compared Nock's general world view with that of Henry Adams. To Brooks, Nock was "a professional exile, a homeless man . . . a scholar gypsy, resembling the two friends of his own youth who had given him 'the curious impression of somehow not belonging where they were.' "[44] Brooks believed that Nock's essay on Rabelais had the same significance to him that *Mont-Saint-Michel et Chartres* had for Henry Adams. To a limited extent, this notion was correct. There was, however, one important distinction to be made. Adams longed for the time when the Virgin symbolized the unity of the world, and when man grew up less convinced than he of the impossibility of acquiring an adequate or meaningful education. It was a longing for a time, a place, and a condition. Nock's longing was less temporal than personal. His affection was for Rabelais the man, not Rabelais the sixteenth century Frenchman who felt, or did not feel, at home in his world. Nock knew he would have been just as out of place in Rabelais's France as he was in twentieth century America. But so, perhaps, would Adams have been.

v

Nock's devotion to the French physician carried over into a delightful travel book, *A Journey into Rabelais's France*, the record of several of Nock's trips (although written as one trip) through areas lived in or described by Rabelais. The book was profusely illustrated by his friend Ruth Robinson, and was one of the more attractive publishing achievements of a depression-ridden industry. Four parts of the text had appeared earlier in the *Bookman*.

Besides the continual crotchety commentary in which Nock excelled, the book was most notable as an expression of its author's views about the good life. Nock's distaste for much of modern life showed in his preferences for the most unspoiled and unvisited places on his itinerary. He made no pretense about the values which the past, immortalized in these places, had for him. "One cannot live happily or even decently without the romance and poetry of existence," he wrote," and since the present world affords so little practicable material for them, one must draw upon the resources that one has laid up in the past."

Nock believed that "one gets most out of travel by starting with a strong interest in some one historical figure," and the book was a development of this theme. He visited Poitiers, Chinon, Toulouse, Port Cros, and the other areas bearing a relation to Rabelais. Civilization rather than Rabelais was the real topic of the book, however, and the proper outlook on life provided by Rabelais and, incidentally, by the modern Frenchman, the book's hero, whose credo was "What the French really stand out against is the idea that men can live by *things* alone—things that are made to sell, and sold for a profit—and that if he can only never have enough things, he will be really happy."[45]

VI

"It would require less than the fingers of the two hands to enumerate those who, from Plato down, rank with Henry George among the world's social philosophers," John Dewey once wrote. Yet one hundred years after George's birth, when Nock wrote *Henry George: An Essay*, George could be called the "Forgotten Man of Anglo–American civilization." Nock's book, along with his previous essays on George, was an attempt to examine George, assess him and his contribution, and find out why his reputation had suffered such an eclipse.

Nock found George to be "unquestionably one of the three or four great constructive statesmen of the nineteenth century, perhaps of any century—he ranks with Turgot." His public character was spotless, he was serious, courageous, and "so sincere as to force even his enemies, of whom he had a great many, to speak well of him." But unfortunately, in Matthew Arnold's terminology, he was Hebraic. "He had absolutely no sense of humour. He was as humourless as Oliver Cromwell, a born crusader of the Old Testament type, convinced that he had an Old Testment mission to hew Agag to pieces."[46]

Nock could have little personal affection for such a person, as he had for Jefferson or Rabelais. The great thing about George was not what he was, but what he wrote. His work was not original, although he discovered it without help. Turgot had set forth the principle which George used to formulate his law of wages, although again George did not know it. George's "great merit is that of having worked out his discovery to its full logical length in a complete system, which none of his predecessors did." Not only did he establish fundamental economics as a true science, he also discovered and clearly marked out "its natural relations with history, politics and ethics."[47]

Nock traced Henry George from his belligerently philistine environment through his years of poverty in San Francisco. At first a believer in the "ethic of Murdstone," the faith in work and the belief that all who are good can rise by hard labor, George gradually became disillusioned when his hard labor brought no commensurate reward. This story, however, has been retold many times and need not be repeated here. What should be noted was the reason for the failure of George's philosophy.

Nock put his case succinctly:

> The key to an understanding of George's career may be found in the story that Lincoln Steffens tells about an afternoon ride with the devil on the top of a Fifth Avenue bus. The devil was in uncommonly good spirits that day, and entertained Steffens with a fine salty line of reminiscences half way up the avenue, when Steffens suddenly caught sight of a man on the sidewalk who was carefully carrying a small parcel of truth. Steffens nudged the devil, who gave the man a casual glance, but kept on talking, apparently not interested. When Steffens could get a word in, he said, "See here, didn't you notice that that man back there had got hold of a little bit of truth?"
>
> "Yes, of course I noticed it." replied the devil. "Why?"
>
> "But surely that's a very dangerous thing," Steffens said. "Aren't you going to do something about it?"
>
> "No hurry, my dear fellow," the devil answered indulgently. "It's a simple matter. I'll be running across him again one of these days, and I'll get him to organize it."[48]

Here again, Nock's individualism guided his analysis. Any good thing, he felt, could be taken, organized, and made into a stifling orthodoxy, in the end destroying whatever good had inhered in the thing. This had been the course with democracy, Christianity, and now with Henry George and his ideas. Had George eschewed politics and contented himself with doing nothing but formulating and speaking the truth, Nock felt he would have been far more successful.

Despite George's failure in politics and his own abandonment of the environmentalist postulate of human perfectibility, Nock retained his affection for George throughout his life. George, at heart, had been an anarchist, attempting to create a society without a state. Nock was devoted to minimum government. Provided one could accept this change, from the idea that government will eventually be unnecessary to the idea that it is a necessary evil, George's philosophy would enable people "to improve themselves up to the limit of their psychical capacity, whatever that may be."[49] In other words, Nock felt that men need not be perfect or perfectible to live in a Spencerian society or a modified Georgian society; but without this freedom of perfectibility they could not be as good, as humane, as they might be.

Nock also emphasized that the later quarrel between George and Spencer did not affect the validity of the *Social Statics* and *Progress and Poverty*. The later Spencer was not a classical liberal but a testy obscurantist, and Nock would have none of this. The whole quarrel, he thought, was "simply so much clear evidence of the supreme silliness of making a system of philosophy the subject matter of public controversy or a campaign of propaganda." Even if the two men disavowed every line of their great works (something Spencer just about did), the validity of their ideas would remain unimpaired. Nor did the acceptance of the doctrines by any large number of people matter. As long as the books were available and intelligent men could read them, the ideas would remain ready for the time, however distant, when the ideas could be translated into realities. Majority rule could make truth only if might made right; this was the ultimate perversion of the democratic dogma.[50]

The reviews of *Henry George* were mixed. Most reviewers acknowledged the brilliance of Nock's style, while attacking either his view of Henry George as a significant philosopher or his view that minimum government was the preferred form of social structure. The New Deal and the Popular Front had influenced critics a great deal, and many of them used political rather than literary or historical criteria. The book remains the least remembered and admired biography Nock did, although retaining numerous admirers.

VII

Henry George the philosopher, Artemus Ward the critic, Jefferson the libertarian practitioner of taste and manners, and Rabelais, with his certain jollity of mind, pickled in the scorn of fortune, were the subjects of Nock's biographical views. In general, the books were objective essays into the mind and personality of the subject, rather than mere collections of fact and anecdote. Although his economic and political views popped up disconcertingly at times, the books were, on the whole, objective, and generally well received. At least one, *Jefferson*, has achieved the status of a minor classic and is still in print, read, and admired by students and teachers alike.

CHAPTER EIGHT

THEORETICAL REFORMULATIONS; EDUCATION

Aɴʏ attempt at scholarship sharpens thinking; it enables a man to examine origins and influences, causes and effects in the lives of others. Through this examination, the scholar can appraise his own views, re-examine his positions, and mature intellectually. Nock's examination of the past helped to round out his education in the events since 1500, where his education had stopped. Rabelais introduced him to the origins of the issues faced by modern Europe; Jefferson, Artemus Ward, and Henry George gave him a thorough grounding in American history. As the thirties dawned in depression gray, Nock moved toward the major change in his philosophy.

Matthew Arnold's notion of *humanity* as the exceptional few taken from the ranks of the barbarians, the philistines, and the populace, including parts of the characters of these latter people which training could bring out, prepared Nock's mind for an increasing élitism. The term Nock used throughout much of his discussion was "Remnant" rather than "humanity," but the first was but a logical development from the second. The term "Remnant" appeared in Nock's work as early as 1924, in the essay "Artemus Ward." These people, the Remnant, were those who possessed *Intelligenz*; they were the hope of society. Jefferson may have been Nock's ideal man, but John Adams turned out to be the theorist whose pessimism proved most prophetic.

As early as September 10, 1932, Nock wrote in his journal that he thought the purely zoological classification of human beings incorrect. Not everyone, he remarked, "who answers to *homo sapiens* is human; relatively few are." A greater gulf separated Socrates, Marcus Aurelius, or Sophocles from the man in the crowd than separated him from the higher anthropoids. Despite this fact, Socrates was no better than the man in the crowd to most people. "This line of thought was suggested to me by Dr. McConnell's little book called *Immortality*—an extraordinary piece of work. I am not trained in science, so I cannot say how sound its science is; but I am immensely impressed with it."[1]

Almost simultaneously, in the September *American Mercury,* Ralph Adams Cram developed his own version of this theory, integrated into a philosophy of history. Nock later pointed to Cram's essay, when he wished to show the crucial turning point in his own thought. Cram's article, "Why We Do Not Behave Like Human Beings," caused Nock to write two essays, in *Harper's* and the *Atlantic,* thinking out loud about Cram before he finally took the hypothesis for his own. He did not say flatly that Cram was right; he said that Cram's theory explained things that were hitherto inexplicable, and that until a better explanation came along Cram's would have to do.

Cram began by demolishing Spencer's *Synthetic Philosophy,* with its nineteenth century faith in inevitable progress and perfectible man. Society to Cram, far from progressing, had remained static in its biological capabilities since Neolithic times. *In toto,* mankind had improved only its resources and its fund of knowledge; it had not improved its ability to deal with this knowlege. Progress was the result of the work of a few geniuses, plus this accumulated knowledge. The modern average man had outward trappings of democracy and thousands of years of written record, but at birth and by nature he was no better than his Greek or Cretan ancestor. Mankind, in modern terms, came into existence in the Neolithic period, and in a few spurts achieved a great civilization. This died, to be revived during the Renaissance. The revival was due to the geniuses, the circumstances, coincidences, or other phenomena, but not to any improvement in man as raw material. The geniuses, which one thought of erroneously as typical guides for the term "human being," were the result not of meliorism but of catastrophe. Cram thought that de Vries was right when he claimed that evolution occurred not after the Darwinian fashion, always from lower to higher and by the constant accretion of minute differences, but by the catastrophic process: "the periodical and unaccountable appearance, in the midst of many type forms, of one that is entirely new. In some cases this new thing reproduces itself true to form, and indefinitely; in others there is an ultimate reversion to type."[2]

In connection with these developments, a law of history explained the role both of geniuses and the masses; the genius began the cycle of inventive talent, and no organized means repressed his abilities. His work improved the lot of all. Eventually mass man, through politics and the sheer weight of numbers, so burdened the inventive character as to make impossible further creative work, the political means expropriating the economic means. Unable to sustain themselves under the increasing weight of the political means, the geniuses gave up and society gradually collapsed of its own weight. "By some mysterious terrestrial law," Cram hypothesized, "the rhythm of history beats in great throbs of five centuries." One could trace this back in time as far as old Egypt. "Each era describes a curve," varying in many ways, but "inevitable." The line of each new rise often overlapped the decline of the old, but each in itself followed this pattern. "As the trajectory of our own epoch rose as hissingly as a rocket about fifteen hundred to its apogee about nineteen hundred, so its fall begins as again a rocket falls, and the first overt showing of this change of direction was the Great War."[3]

Throughout these periods, atrocities, depravity, ignorance, and bigotry reoccurred on one hand. Yet, at the same time, a consistent record of the reoccurrence of genius appeared: ". . . there never has been a time when out of the darkness did not flame into light bright figures of men and women who in character and capacity were a glory to the human race. . . ." Cram came to the conclusion, as Nock had noted in his journal, that between the great man and the mass of men, "there was a difference greater than that which separates, shall we say, the obscene mob of the November Revolution in Russia, and the anthropoid apes. They fall into two absolutely different categories . . . which is precisely the point I wish to make."[4]

Even the beloved Rabelais had hinted at this solution. At the request of Friar John, the Abbey of Thélème was to be instituted "contrary to all others." Whatever was done in other convents and monasteries, the opposite was to be done at Thélème: men and women would live together, only good looking women would be admitted, no clocks would be allowed, nor would there be time requirements for services. The Thélèmites were a superior breed, no matter how defined. Cram had given this utopia a quasi-scientific underpinning; the cultivation of Thélèmites, of the Remnant, was thus the only way for a society to preserve itself. The pessimism implied in the writing of Cram, Nock, and others of this school came from their belief that mass man would never consent to living so as to encourage the Remnant. Mass man was incapable of seeing that this was the only way to stave off the otherwise inevitable cycle of history.

Nock devoted one of his best essays, "Isaiah's Job," to his discussion of the concept of the Remnant. In it, one can find considerable evidence of how Nock felt about his role as a commentator on the affairs of men. Isaiah began his career at the end of King Uzziah's reign, about 740 B.C. The reign had been quite long, and very prosperous. As in the reigns of Marcus Aurelius, Eubulus of Athens, or Calvin Coolidge, however, prosperity had petered out quickly, and depression followed. The year Uzziah died, the Lord commissioned Isaiah to go out and warn the people of the wrath to come. He instructed Isaiah to tell them how worthless they were, what was wrong, why, and what was going to happen to them if they did not reform. But, He added, He thought He should warn Isaiah that it would not do any good. "The official class and their intelligentsia will turn up their noses at you, and the masses will not even listen. They will all keep on in their own ways until they carry everything down to destruction, and you will probably be lucky if you get out with your life."

Isaiah had been eager for the job, but this advice dampened his ardor. Why bother, he asked, if failure was ordained? Because, the Lord answered, "there is a Remnant there that you know nothing about." Its members were obscure, unorganized, inarticulate. They were discouraged and they needed support, "because when everything has gone completely to the dogs, they are the ones who will come back and build up a new society, and meanwhile your preaching will reassure them and keep them hanging on. Your job is to take care of the Remnant. . . ."[5] In the Remnant were no qualifications except merit. Money or social position made no difference whatsoever, just as it did not matter with Arnold, Rabelais, Jefferson, or Cram. Take care of the quality, and the quantity will profit more, in the long run, than if they were taken care of at the expense of the quality.

The trouble with twentieth century America was that Isaiah's job was going begging. No one was taking care of the Remnant. Everyone measured success by numbers, not by quality. Taking something to the masses for their approval was an example of the degradation of the democratic dogma, a capitulation to the idea that numbers could create truth. Because most people could not, or would not apprehend truths which they disliked, most messages to them were watered down to innocuous vacuity. This did not change the masses, since it only hardened their prejudices. Meanwhile, "the Remnant, aware of this adulteration and of the desires that prompt it, turn their backs on the prophet and will have nothing to do with him or his message."[6] The most immediate example was the case of Henry George.

On the other hand, the man who, like Isaiah, tended only to the Remnant and did not adulterate his message always found his audience, and because his audience was of his level, his message was pure. The prophet of the Remnant, Nock wrote, "is in the enviable position of Papa Haydn in the household of Prince

Esterhazy. All Haydn had to do was to keep forking out the very best music he knew how to produce, knowing it would be understood and appreciated by those for whom he produced it, and caring not a button what anyone else thought of it; and that makes a good job."[7] No matter what the circumstances, the man doing Isaiah's job knew but two things about the Remnant: "first, that they exist; second, that they will find you." A man who cultivated his own garden well need never worry about an audience. Nock devoted himself to doing just that.

II

A modern Isaiah should be familiar with three aspects of human life. Like Henry Adams, Nock made up certain laws which he saw governing human events. One was borrowed from Henry George, the others from science and economics. All were applied to phenomena that their original formulators would not have guessed at.

The first was called "Epstean's law," after Nock's friend Edward Epstean, who, Nock said, had first given him the idea of its application: "I tell you," Epstean had said, "if self-preservation is the first law of conduct, exploitation is the second." Nock pounced on the remark. Spencer and George had familiarized him with the formula that man always tended to satisfy his need and desires with the least possible exertion, but had given him no hint of the vast area in which the law applied. "Indeed, if one wished to split hairs, one might say that exploitation is the first law of conduct, since even in self-preservation one tends always to take the easiest way. . . ." Epstean's law, then, read "Man tends to satisfy his needs and desires with the least possible exertion."[8]

The other two laws were Gresham's law, that bad money drives out good, and Newton's law of diminishing returns. Armed with these three laws, Nock was ready once again to venture forth into the worlds of education, morals, politics, and the good life. When he came to analyze the decline in literary standards that had taken place in America over the past fifty years, he had only to say that bad literature drives out good: "The current value of literature is determined by the worst type of literature in circulation." Thus Americans had *Ben Hur* and Bruce Barton, while the Adams-Jefferson letters remained uncollected. Publishers, faced with the demands of a mass market, could often print only that which would make the most money. Since the best material rarely found a mass market, the best material was published only at a loss. Education, on the other hand, ran aground on the law of diminishing returns. The more students, the lower the median of intelligence, and thus the lower the standards. In many classrooms, the least common denominator set the pace, if "pace" is the correct expression. Democracy ran aground on Epstean's law: why should people use the economic means, when the political means required less exertion? Further, the law of diminishing returns worked against any large political organization being of value. The best democracies—Greek or Swiss—were also the smallest. People could watch and control them, and dispose of the parasites eating by political means. In a large, centralized country, no such control was possible, and the quality of everything deteriorated when the seat of power shifted.[9]

III

The first area in which Nock applied his laws, and in which the Cram thesis played a major role, was education. He had long been interested in educational theory, and had written sporadically over the years on the subject. To the civilized man, education was the means of obtaining joy, of cultivating one's joy-finding faculties. Always his own peculiar form of hedonist, Nock emphasized repeatedly that Americans, surrounded by more means of enjoyment than any other people in history, nevertheless never seemed to have a good time. The trouble was that Pantagruelian education, formative education in the joys of learning for their own sake, had disappeared in the dreary attempt at absolute utility which Dewey and his disciples had foisted on the country. A campaign against Dewey, Nock wrote, should begin with "a violent frontal assault on the enemy's whole theory of life." If the world was really a place only for work, if Murdstone's nemesis, moping and droning, was not to be allowed, then Dewey and the vocationalists had the true theory. But, Nock complained, the world is no such thing, "it is a place to have fun in," and "you can have ten times more fun and better fun throughout your life if you know Greek and Latin literature, and the more intimately you know it and the closer you stick to it, the more fun you will have." Far from being a secondary purpose, joy was life's primary object, and the classics should be taken in this vein. Let no one apologize, or admit the opponent's case by saying that Latin study makes better carpenters. Such an approach was utilitarian, and the classics could not be looked at in this way except as useful for the whole life, the life of joy.[10]

In 1930, Abraham Flexner published *Universities: American, English, German*, the first substantial hardcover salvo at the vocationalists. A year later, Nock delivered his Page–Barbour lectures, and H. H. Horne published *This New Education*. In 1932, Nock's lectures were published as *The Theory of Education in the United States*, and Sister J. M. Raby put forth a Roman Catholic view similar to Nock's in *A Critical Study of the New Education*. Others followed in later years, the most eminent of which were Robert Maynard Hutchins' *The Higher Learning in America* and later books, Mark Van Doren's *Liberal Education*, and Jacques Maritain's *Education at the Crossroads*.

The crucial point in Nock's thought on education was the distinction between "educable" and "trainable," and without careful definition of these terms all his writings on education seemed greatly distorted. The educable person was one who was capable of absorbing and profiting from formative knowledge. The trainable person was one who was capable of profiting only from instrumental knowledge. "Education, properly applied to suitable material, produces something in the way of an Emerson;

while training, properly applied to suitable material, produces something in the way of an Edison."[11]

In other words, science was training, not education. The scientific genius should take up his field within school hours only after having been given a formative education if he wished to achieve the status of an educated man.

> If education contemplates intelligence and wisdom—and what else can it contemplate—one who for years had been President of a notable college for women must surely have perceived that the vast majority of his students were ineducable. He could do great things for them in the way of biologists, botanists, geologists, chemists, perhaps even passable cooks and housekeepers if his institution carried the requisite equipment; he could make them good grammarians, philologists, even historians, all of a psittacine type; but educate them he could not.[12]

Nock's definition was unacceptable to a great number of his critics, who cringed at the thought of eminent men who could thus be termed ineducable. Many of these critics misunderstood his meaning.

Nock thought that the trouble with the American theory of education was that it did not, and by its very nature could not, produce educated men. This was true because the theory was based on specious reasoning, myth, and error: "Our system is based upon the assumption, popularly regarded as implicit in the doctrine of equality, that everybody is educable. This has been taken without question from the start; it is taken without question now [1931]."[13] All our laws were based on this premise, for in these laws emphasis was placed not on ability but on age, thus assuming equal ability. Yet when one attempted to find out the origins of this erroneous belief he could not, for never had such a philosophical doctrine in America been postulated by eminent men: "The philosophical doctrine of equality gives no more ground for the assumption that all men are educable than it does for the assumption that all men are six feet tall. We see at once, then, that it is not the philosophical doctrine of equality, but an utterly untenable popular perversion of it, that we find at the basis of our educational system."[14] Nock went on to support this statement with quotations from Jefferson, who was often thought of as the seminal thinker in the field of public education. Nock, with other historians, believed that what Jefferson had in mind was the system which had been inaugurated in France. He thought there was some historical evidence to show that, in fact, Jefferson had had an important role in moulding the French system.

The second error in educational thought lay in the concept of democracy, which Nock termed "a perversion upon a perversion." America was not a democracy at all, but a republic, and the distinction was more than a mere semantical problem. In a democracy, everyone voted on all issues and the majority ruled. In a republic, representatives were selected to cast ballots for constituents, but because everyone could vote for these representatives, the term "democratic" became popularly synonymous with "republican." True democracy was strictly an economic condition. In its purest form, it would be a doctrine of public property. Those that voted did not rule; those that owned did, and suffrage could be extended to every living creature without changing the actual rulership of the country. Republicanism did not, "of itself even imply democracy." A great many people were aware that some monarchies were much more forward in democracy than some republics, even republics with universal suffrage. "The antithesis of republicanism is monarchy," but "monarchy is not the antithesis of democracy. The antithesis of democracy is absolutism, and absolutism may, and notoriously does, prevail under a republican regime as freely as under any other."[15]

This was the first confusion, or "perversion." The second was "the popular error which accepted as democratic whatever was merely indiscriminate." A common tendency in America was to label a person as having democratic manners when he was only affable, or even only coarse or crude. Democratic manners did not exist. Manners were either good or bad. "A man thinks to show himself my equal by showing himself *grob*," Heine wrote,

"he does not show himself my equal; he shows himself *grob*."
A society that thought otherwise could easily confuse quality
with quantity, the good and the common. Discrimination was a
necessary trait, a trait that many Americans had lost.[16]

Nock was careful to distinguish between motive and effect
in his discussion, for he realized that the root of the theory, despite the failure of the theory, was a part of the American dream.
He realized the difficulty of attacking the position of people
who meant well. At the root of the theory "lay one of the most
humane, honourable and engaging sentiments that are in the
power of human nature to generate or to indulge"—the sentiment which prompted the pioneers to hope that their children
could have a better life, a more humane and civilized life, than
the one that circumstances forced them to lead. Yet the
interpretation of this sentiment "frequently betrays a vast ignorance of what the humane life really is, and of the discipline
whereby alone one may make progress toward this life."[17]

Unfortunately, the popular mind was not receptive to the
compatibility of both the doctrine of equality, and the plain fact
that some are more able than others. When one person appeared
more able, others regarded this not as ability but as conceit.
"The popular idea of democracy is animated by a very strong
resentment of superiority. It resents the thought of an élite; the
thought that there are practical ranges of intellectual and spiritual experience, achievement and enjoyment, which by nature
are open to some and not to all." The egalitarian deprecated this
thought, and discouraged it whenever he could. Just as the popular idea of equality postulated that "in the realm of the spirit
everybody is able to enjoy everything that anybody can enjoy,"
so the popular idea of democracy postulated that "there shall be
nothing worth enjoying for anybody to enjoy that everybody
may not enjoy." Anyone thinking and saying anything to the
contrary was immediately exposed "to all the evils of a dogged,
unintelligent, invincibly suspicious resentment."[18] Thus public
education in America reflected these popular misconceptions of

equality and democracy. Education, so-called, was leveled at the capacity of the lowest common denominator.

The third idea in the American theory was "the idea that good government and a generally wholesome public order are conditioned upon having a literate citizenry. . . ." This was an idea dear to Jefferson, and one for which Nock criticized his favorite. The major defect in this concept was the false belief that literacy and the ability to read were synonymous. People were much more able to pass things through their minds than they were able to think about them. Because of this, most time spent in reading was a waste of time, since few thought about what they read. One had only to look at literate America to see that the people could not read in any but the most primitive sense: "Remark its intellectual interests, the general furniture of its mind, as those are revealed by what it reads; by the colossal, the unconscionable, volume of garbage annually shot upon the public from the presses of the country. . . ."[19]

Thus the three erroneous doctrines in the American theory were that of democracy, which confused "democratic" with "indiscriminate," and held that there shall be nothing to enjoy for anyone that everybody may not enjoy; that of equality, which prevented proper training of true merit and assumed that equal rights and legal treatment implied equal abilities; and the idea that literacy, the ability to pass print through the mind, was the same as the idea of reading, which implied retention, understanding, and a certain level of ability.

Nock's description of the classical curriculum, his favored educational process, placed him in the vanguard of those wishing a return to the old system. The disciplinary value of the studies he mentioned, but only in passing, since most educators acknowledged this value in the classical curriculum. But what he wished to emphasize was the formative character of these studies. The literature of Rome and Greece comprised "the longest and fullest continuous record available to us, of what the human mind had been busy about in practically every department of spiritual and social activity" over a period of twenty-five hundred years. The mind that had read and absorbed this literature was "not only a disciplined mind but an *experienced* mind; a mind that instinctively views a contemporary phenomenon from the vantage point of an immensely long perspective attained through this profound and weighty experience of the human spirit's operations." These studies were also formative because they were "*maturing*, because they powerfully inculcate the views of life and the demands on life that are appropriate to maturity and that are indeed the specific marks, the outward and visible signs, of the inward and spiritual grace of maturity." The process of experience, the process of maturation, was the formative result of the classical curriculum properly administered, "and the constant aim at inculcation of these views and demands is what we know under the name of the Great Tradition of our republic."[20]

What happened in America was that educators tried to give a taste of the Great Tradition to everyone, and this proved futile. "The reason it did not work was that this process postulated an educable person, and everybody is not educable." Here arose the conflict between the democratic–equalitarian ideals and the hard facts. Experience clashed with good intentions and theory, and broached a serious dilemma for education. "We had, then, the choice of revising our theory, or of letting it stand and sophisticating our practice into some sort of correspondence with it."[21] America chose to retain the theory and change the practice, and was the field for dozens of competing explanatory theories, none of which solved anything.

The distinction between education and training was first drawn by Ernest Renan when he said that the United States had set up "a considerable popular instruction without any serious higher education." Most people were able to absorb instrumental training and unable to absorb the formative education of the Great Tradition. Since anyone could be trained and the specious democratic theory demanded a process that everyone could profit from, the salvation of the theory of education in the United

States was to call training "education." The theory would not have to be changed at all if this were done. The American dream could remain intact, even though the children of the pioneers were receiving only training and not education.

The first move Nock recommended was to recognize the distinction between training and education. Most American schools were excellently set up for training. Their character would change little; their graduates would merely be regarded as trained and not educated—that was the change. Henry Ford, in his school for boys at Sudbury, had provided an excellent pilot project for what Nock intended. There Ford took boys and trained them without a bow in the direction of the Great Tradition. "In this I think he is precisely right." All institutions should do this, and stop the absurd attempt to educate those who could only be trained.[22]

A corollary to this change was the need for accurate descriptions of institutions and degrees. "Institutes" rather than "universities" would be distinguishing without being demeaning, as a name for the higher institutions for the trainable; a degree other than the B.A. would be awarded the institute graduate. By this means the functions of training and education would not disrupt each other, and the law of bad money driving out good and the law of diminishing returns would not be able to wreak havoc with education.

But honesty in nomenclature, while useful, was not the only reason for effecting these few changes in American education. For one group, no place was open in American institutions; that was the tragedy of the system. The educable person was socially valuable and a potential asset to any country, and "our system does not, and by the conditions of its theory cannot, do anything whereby we can realize on their value. They simply go to waste, and as matters stand, they must do so."[23]

The care and nurture of the Great Tradition and the educable person were at the heart of Nock's educational philosophy, for the educable person had the means of attaining the good life, joy, and humanity. He could point the way to others less fortunate, who might have a few of the qualities necessary. He was a member of the élite that Jefferson thought his yeomen could recognize and elect, even if they could not belong themselves. This educable person, "in contrast to the ineducable, is one who gives promise of some day being able to think," and the object of educating him under the discipline of the Great Tradition "is to put him in the way of right thinking, mature and profound thinking." This was so important because "all the progress in actual civilization that society has ever made has been brought about, not by machinery, not by political programmes, platforms, parties, not even by revolutions, but by right thinking."[24]

In other words, Nock's conception of social change was that of one who had a profound faith in the idea, one who felt that ideas did have consequences and that without these ideas, correct ideas, the world could not achieve its goals. He believed further than unless the men who led the world could look on its events disinterestedly, could take the long view and sense what Hendrik Willem Van Loon called the "feeling of inevitability" about the world's events, they were doomed to operation by expediency. Such operation was by nature chaotic, and effective only in the short run. Nature had her own laws, and exacted penalties for infractions. The right-thinking man, the man knowledgeable in the Great Tradition, was the only person capable of judging events and informing fellow citizens of what was necessary. One feature of history appeared with unfailing regularity in the course of human activity: "Every social enterprise, every movement, every policy, which was not conceived in right thinking has in the long run cost more than it came to." Nature, an outside force, fate, or whatnot levied a fine on it, "proportioned with interesting precision to the degree of its departure from the counsels of right thinking." No greater lesson could be obtained from the Great Tradition. The idea of a rational and ordered world which so influenced Spencer was vital to Nock's thought. All events had order, meaning. Any society which did not take into account the case of the interpreter of this natural order, who ignored the counsels of the Great Tradition, was taking a considerable risk, "so considerable that in the whole course of human experience, as far as our records go, no society ever yet has taken it without coming to great disaster."[25]

Nock was almost alone, in 1931, in this faith in natural order, and few had his faith in the causative force of ideas. Men who had been moved profoundly by Marx and Engels, who had been ecstatic over and had acted upon the ideas of Dewey, and who were about to cheer a book by John Maynard Keynes, nevertheless touted the act of doing and depreciated the act of thinking. The times demanded action, and action had even become a philosophical postulate. Dewey and James had moved a whole generation to a faith that, if true, would have made it impossible for ideas—and thus its own philosophical idea—to operate successfully. Men who were moved by ideas denied the force of ideas, and ended by justifying their lack of reason and order in the work of Thurman Arnold and in the faith in action and lack of long-range planning, so glorified in *The Folklore of Capitalism*. Expediency had become an orthodoxy as stifling as any orthodoxy it had replaced. Nock retained his nineteenth century faith in order, and was laughed at by the men of action.

IV

But the educational view had one further important aspect, the interrelation of the terms "educable," "Remnant," "élite," and so on. Nock believed in immortality, but only for a few; these few could be labeled by any of the preceding phrases. "I have always had a strong belief that some personalities survive death, though I do not expect my own to do so,"[26] he once wrote Mrs. Evans. Of course, one could never be sure, and there might well be a speculative case to be made for Nock's relation to the Puritan doctrine of the "elect." Stripped of religious pretension, such a doctrine would be indistinguishable from Nock's notion of those who were immortal. The touch of John Calvin seems clammy on the admirer of Rabelais, but it is impossible to escape the conclusion that much of Nock's thought on education, and later on politics and morals, is the secularization of a Puritan dogma: "I see no reason why the vast majority of mankind should survive death, because experience and the intimation of purpose in nature alike present the idea of persistence as an achievement, as a matter of diligent and progressive adaptation to environment. . . ." The simple truth was that ". . . the vast majority are so dead while they live that one may suppose they stay dead when they die." Immortality was closely connected with natural order—Herbert Spencer had become a Jeffersonian élitist: ". . . my intimations of purpose in nature, vague as they may be, are distinctly affronted by the suggestion that certain . . . personalities do not survive death. If Socrates, Marcus Aurelius, Dante, Cervantes, Shakespeare, and Rabelais do not survive death, then, as all my intimations lead me to see it, the order of nature is a most inglorious fizzle."[27]

With these factors in mind, the final passage of the *Theory of Education* takes on the aura of a biblical exhortation. Nock was talking about more than education, even in his special restricted sense. "We are called to be disciples, not energumens." The Great Tradition would go on "because the forces of nature are on its side," and it had an invincible ally, "the self-preserving instinct of humanity." Men could forsake it, but come back to it they would. They had to, for their collective existence could not permanently go on without it. Whole societies might deny it, as America had done, substituting bread and buncombe, power and riches, or expediency; "but in the end, they will find, as so many societies have already found, that they must return and seek the regenerative power of the Great Tradition, or lapse into decay and death."

The Great Tradition would persist even if ignored. It had its own "august and salutary" laws, and man had no further responsibility "but the happy one of keeping our eyes single to our own obedience" to it. Man did not have to worry about the Great Tradition; he had to worry about himself. American society, however, would never return to the Great Tradition. It would repeat the experience of other societies, having gone too far to retrace its steps. But the man of letters had no country, and should seek sustenance elsewhere. "Our fellow citizens are ours where we find them; and where they are not to be found, we may regard ourselves as citizens *in partibus*, uncommitted to an officious and ineffectual evangelism. Our allegiance is to the constitution of our republic; we are committed only to clear understanding and right thinking. . . ."[28] Could it be that another term for the Great Tradition would be God?

The reception of *The Theory of Education in the United States* was understandably mixed. Some, like President Mac-Cracken of Vassar in the *Saturday Review of Literature*, heaped sarcasm and ridicule on the book with the idea that their comments were responsible criticism. Others, like Grenville Vernon in *Commonweal*, found the book delightful, but perhaps a trifle exaggerated and overly pessimistic. The two most illuminating comments came from the two leaders of the opposing movements in American education.

John Dewey devoted three full columns to the book in the *New Republic*. He was both attracted and repelled. "Since anything Mr. Nock writes is worth pondering both for its style . . . and for substance," he wrote, "it is to be hoped that the extreme exaggeration of his book will not repel educators and trainers from giving it serious consideration." Much of Dewey's review dealt with the differences of opinion he had with Nock. He felt that scholars in the Great Tradition had increased rather than decreased, and that the Great Tradition was itself in large measure training. Specifically, he wrote, such training was "largely a vocational preparation for the ministry and for teaching. What has happened is that the number of callings for which schools prepare has greatly multiplied." He felt further that the reforms Nock wished, while worth considering, were too far in the future. What had to be done immediately was to achieve democracy, and Dewey meant the term economically, as Nock did.[29]

Abraham Flexner, in the *Nation*, received the book joyfully. "A small volume on education, worthy in style and content of

Matthew Arnold's pen and brain—is not this an amazing event? It comes, of course, not from a professor in a school or college of education, but from an urbane and mellow scholar, educated in what he calls the Great Tradition, and keenly sensitive to the meaning of words. . . ."[30] Flexner was neither so pessimistic about the future nor as enamored of the classics as Nock, although he admitted that the classics were just as valuable as Nock thought. Flexner believed that the Great Tradition could be sensed through study of nonclassical disciplines without reducing its value. Most modern liberal arts enthusiasts would agree with him.

Increasingly, as the depression turned men toward politics and immediate material results, Nock's view of education was submerged. A few voices—Flexner, Hutchins—kept some of his ideas alive, but not until after the Second World War did the anti-Dewey revolt become formidable. Nock was through with educational theorizing. He had said what he thought, and few listened. Eventually, he too turned to politics for his subject matter. First, however, he concerned himself with women and morals.

CHAPTER NINE

THE SHADOW OF THE TITANESS:

Women and Morals

And meanwhile the Middle Western woman had quietly become a fixture on the American social chart, a shadowy Titaness, a terror to editors, the hope of missionary societies and the prey of lecturers. . . . She was an emblem, a grotesque shape in hot black silk, screaming threats at naked children in a clear river, with her companionable ministers and reformers at heel. The collapse of American thought excused her forays; all that had been finely stalwart in the Bostonian age had vanished, the reckless courage and self-willed individualism of Emerson, Thoreau and Channing, the deliberate cultivation of research into the motives, not the manners of human action. The confusion of morals with manners, apparently inherent in the world that speaks English, had helped the mental lassitude of the Americans to destroy what was honourable in the Bostonian tradition, and from the remains of that tradition welled a perfume of decay, chants and meaningless phrases. . . .

*—*THOMAS BEER[1]

T HE Age of the Titaness, the American version of Victorian England, was the world in which Nock grew up. He was close to his strong-willed and domineering mother, even when developing a moral system that would have shocked her had she understood it. But it was hard to overthrow the weight of an entire age, and the influence of the Titaness, even when she had been outwardly replaced by the legally equal flapper in American life, remained in Nock's writings.

One result of Nock's Victorian upbringing was that he developed a great dislike for two aspects of Victorian America—the comstockian moralist and the censor. Marriage, he wrote, "looks to me a whole heap like an endurance test, and I think it is a pretty humiliating business."[2] It degraded the women, stifled their intellects, and forced men to rely only on other men for intellectual stimulation. Yet when men tried to rectify this state of affairs by cultivating intellectual female companions, a prurient America frowned and disapproved. The explanation might be complicated, but much of this comstockery was a combination of history and physical deprivation. He had, he wrote, "seen a great deal of the kind of lady who is so uncommonly anxious that the rest of the world should be very moral and proper, according to the standard set on Plymouth Rock." He always suspected "that the vices and shortcomings of other people would interest her very much less if four or five times a week the right man should get his arms around under her shoulderblades and make her think she had been caught flat on her back in a hay-press." The same was true of men, for anyone "who has persistently neglected or violated a natural instinct is mighty apt to find it ingrowing into something meaner and dirtier than white slavery. That is the reason why the Puritans, with all their virtues, earned the contempt of normal people."[3]

Censorship was another form of puritanism, an attempt to scare and repress people into doing good. When Ellery Sedgwick, during the First World War, recommended a tax on the use of German words printed in America, Nock sent a scorching letter to his long-time friend. What makes a nation great, he wrote, is "the manner of spirit" it embodies, its "geist" and its "Ernst der ins ganze geht, if you won't tax me two cents apiece for those words before I get my fall crops in." America would never have such a *Geist* if the leaders of opinion like Sedgwick stooped to such absurd pettiness. Hatred begot hatred, he continued, and it was far better to trust in some divine order than truckle to "some little ponderous unhumourous lucubration of a few poor pitiful wretches in Washington, beset and bedeviled as

they are by all the demons of need, greed and vain-glory." Good
men must set a good example and not let the petty concerns of
petty men rule their passions. "Making the world safe for democracy by those means has but one historical parallel, that of Buck
Fanshaw [of Twain's *Roughing It*], who was a man of peace and
would have peace if some one had to be carried out on a shutter."[4]

But most of Nock's writing stressed what could and should be
done, rather than what should not be done. The role of women
in society was one that often drew his attention, and appeared
even in works that would seem to have little relation to feminism.
The views of Jefferson and Rabelais on women held Nock's attention longer and more often than they might otherwise have.
In the days before and during the *Freeman* period, Nock periodi-
cally gave the campaigners for equal rights for women an ap-
proving nod, but he never actively campaigned for their cause.
He thought that they had an excellent case and that they should
win it, but that the net effect of a victory would be nugatory.
If those who owned were those who ruled, then the ballot had
but trifling value. Equality was meaningless if civilization were
not improved.

Two ways of expressing appreciation of feminine qualities
were open to men in the twenties. They could ape their Victorian forbears, and put the Titaness on a pedestal as the untouch-
able symbol of purity and goodness, or they could express their
admiration by granting full equality to a creature who deserved
it, ending the double standard of morality and regarding women
as human beings rather than as sexual icons. The two attitudes
were related, and the result of similar emotions: the feeling that
women possessed some quality, aside from their physical nature,
which men did not possess.

Nock first pointed out the increasing wealth owned by women
in the United States. Widows, trustees, wives on allowance all
controlled more wealth than ever before, and the proportion was
increasing. These women were, in other words, increasingly independent economically. Because of this they could assert themselves and obtain their desires, since economic independence

was the *sine qua non* of successful action. To Nock, women's abilities in many fields were demonstrably equal to men's, and their increasing economic leverage would allow them to prove it.

The legacy of the Titaness was evident in his next remarks. Granted, he wrote, that women could be the equals of men in virtually every field, one field was theirs alone. Their duty was to concentrate their efforts in that field. In any society, "the status of what goes on in the realm of the spirit, is the measure of that society's actual civilization." Men seemed concerned mainly with workmanship, with business. This concern could not civilize. Women must bring in "a balanced and harmonious exercise of the instinct of intellect and knowledge, of religion and morals, of beauty and poetry, of social life and manners."[5] Matthew Arnold had acclaimed the balance of Hebraism and Hellenism in the attainment of culture. Culture was the "study of perfection," the pursuit of total perfection of the self by getting to know "the best which has been thought and said in the world." Just this was the advantage of women. They could perceive the balance better than men. They tended less to extremes, and had no driving affection for workmanship and business success. The woman had a special role: she "can civilize a society, and men can not."[6]

This idea was a direct descendant of Victorian notions, without the hypocrisy and anti-intellectuality of the Titaness. Woman's place was not on a pedestal but in society actively promoting qualities which men were unwilling to cultivate. If women were to adopt this task of civilization, perhaps society could last. As things stood, overemphasis on material gains was overwhelming other qualities.

The task for women, then, was to civilize society. The way to do this was to improve one's inward qualities so that one's self was as civilized in outlook as was possible. Nothing, really, could be done in the sense of action; a great deal could be done in the sense of mental preparation and training. Nock's hedonism came out again here in his appreciation for the sense of well-developed civilizing instincts, none of which were out of proportion—essentially a modern version of the Greek devotion to proportion.

"I am not acquainted with anyone who is happy," Edison said on one of his birthdays, and just that was the trouble with the United States. The instinct of workmanship was given importance out of all proportion, other necessary qualities suffered, and civilized qualities atrophied from lack of use.[7]

II

The case of John Stuart Mill provides a good parallel to the biographical background of Nock's ideas on freedom and morals. Mill lived in a period when the eccentric nonconformity of pre-Victorian England was slowly being crushed by the English version of Beer's Titaness "with her companionable ministers and reformers at heel." Convention was becoming rigid code, and hypocrisy a religious duty. Mill felt that a genius could live by his own rules, and that these were rarely if ever the same as society's. His period was one where endless meddling was condoned on moral grounds, blue laws were regarded as God's will, and nonconformity looked upon as alarming and evil.

Mill believed that the creative individual—quite similar to a member of Nock's élite or Remnant—was the only instrument for attaining progress. Such an individual needed wide latitude for experimentation. Just such latitude was denied by Victorian society. One of Mill's habits was to seek the companionship of intelligent women such as his Mrs. Taylor, and these ventures were regarded by the prurient public as immoral, and subject to legal restraint. To Mill, such incursions were indefensible since, first, they had no moral basis in actual fact, and second, since such freedom was necessary to the creative individual, and hence to the social good. Society was incapable of judging the actions of eccentric-seeming people; therefore, they should leave them alone.

Other aspects of Mill's philosophy need not be discussed here. The important parallels to the thought of Nock lay in Mill's ideas about the genius and his need for complete moral freedom, and in Nock's biographical background of female companionship.

Nock, married in 1900, lived with his wife and two children continuously until he joined the staff of the *American Magazine*. He had an eye for a good ankle, as one of his friends puts it, but he concentrated on other interests. Women, in their role as civilizer of society, had something to offer men which other men could not. Nock sought them out on this basis, and enjoyed many lasting relationships with women who seemed intellectually stimulating. He described his feelings just before he died.

> No woman's attraction for me has even been primarily libidinous, nor ever remained purely so. The interest stirred by what we call sex-appeal never affected me. I am a great admirer of woman's physical beauty, as I am of the objects in a jeweller's window; I look at both in the spirit of a delighted connoisseurship, with not the least desire of possession; indeed, the free offer of possession would be most embarrassing. What attracts me to women in the first instance is the display of physical qualities combined with a force of intellect sufficient to carry men and make them effective. This combination is not often found, especially in our American society; and when it exists it is too often vitiated by sex-consciousness. As a rule, American and English women seem to me morbidly conscious of their sex.
>
> Where it is found at its free best, however . . . the ensuing relationship simply reduces physical possession to what seems to me to be its proper level in the scale of importance, as something to be undertaken or not as the progress of the relationship shall determine. . . . The aim of a free association between men and women is the enhancement of physical values and the conservation of romance, beauty, and poetry in human existence.[8]

III

Marriage, to Nock and many nineteenth century liberals before him, was a contract no different from any other. It was an exchange of economic support for desired satisfaction. Should one side or the other wish to terminate the contract, for whatever reason, the only requirement he need fulfill was to support any third parties who might have been conceived from the relationship and had to be brought up. Marriage was "comparable to an exclusive long-time contract for regular deliveries." Woman, like man, needs bread first of all, and "she contracts to get it in perpetuity by regularly exchanging some commodity that man, in obedience to his second fundamental need, finds desirable." The relation is that of merchant and customer, and only the "higgling of the market" proves one or the other more astute.[9]

Woman the marriage merchant was not exactly the topping on the pedestal desired by the Titaness. Yet in so treating women, Nock was according them a respect and faith that no Victorian gentleman would have. The belief that women were too capable to need protection was a compliment of the highest order.

In morals, Nock took a position similar to Mill's. The Remnant had the ability to help and direct civilization, and only they had this ability. To exercise their function, they needed absolute moral freedom—what I call "moral anarchism." To such men as Nock and Mill, the right to be wrong was vitally necessary to a determination of the knowledge of the right, and any restraint not absolutely necessary was an impediment to truth. Thus the only outer restraint allowable was the protection of others from harm—the one law, that of the legendary King Pausole: "Hurt no man, then do as you will." Such was the atmosphere of the Abbey of Thélème; such was the atmosphere Mill thought necessary for his genius. Censorship and sumptuary or morals legislation could have no place in such a world, for they only harmed the civilizing instincts in man. Such an atmosphere as this was abhorrent to the prurient Titaness.

Nock enumerated his views on morals more fully in the title piece of his book, *On Doing The Right Thing*. In this essay, he described the British habit—one of the few British habits for which he had any sympathy—of considering certain acts as things that "aren't done." He divided human conduct into three areas. The first was "the region in which conduct is controlled by law, *i.e.*, by force," or by some form of compulsion. In this area a man could not murder or steal because others would make life difficult for him if he did. Second, "there is the region of indifferent choice," where a person might choose one product on sale over another. Third, "there is the region where conduct is controlled by unenforced, self-imposed allegiance to moral or social considerations." In this region, the individual takes care of "women and children first," does not divulge harmful information about another, and feels called upon to offer food to the starving before eating himself. Because the area for the exercise of these three kind of actions is constant—that is, there are a certain number of acts which can be governed, one way or another—one area can increase only at the expense of the others.[10]

What Nock wished to attack was the ever-increasing tendency to overlegislate, to cure all so-called evils by law and not by social means. The state was, by its nature, simply unable to perform as some people hoped it would. As Herbert Spencer wrote, it was one thing to secure an environment where each man could pursue the good peacefully; it was widely different to pursue that good for him. To do the first efficiently, the state had merely to prevent one person from infringing upon the freedom of others, to maintain machinery of justice, and then stay out of the way. To do the other, "it must become an ubiquitous worker—must know each man's needs better than he knows them himself—must, in short, possess superhuman power and intelligence."[11] The state could be no more than the sum of the people within it, and could not be considered any less fallible than its members. The point Nock wished to make was that, whether a law was good, bad, or ineffectual, "any enlargement, good or bad, reduces the scope of individual responsibility, and thus retards and cripples the education which can be a product of nothing but the free exercise of moral judgment."[12]

This was the core of Nock's moral anarchism. People could mature and develop their faculties only if they were required to use them. As soon as the state pre-empted this use by taking over functions that could be accomplished by private effort, the urge and ability to act on the part of each person began to atrophy, and the people became less competent to handle their own problems. Philosophical anarchism as a political creed has been rightly dismissed because of its dependence on the basic perfection or ultimate perfectibilty of man—as in Henry George, Jefferson, Lester Ward, Rousseau, and Nock in earlier years.

But no such difficulty existed in the moral realm, since there men need act only for themselves. Basic goodness was irrelevant. No one could impose his ethical imperatives on another. He could by political power enforce outward conformity or prohibit by law certain exercises of a man's ethical beliefs, but he could not force his beliefs on others. In this essay, one reason for Nock's disenchantment with the ministry is clear. He could not allow himself to forfeit his right to think and decide for himself about an orthodoxy, no matter how well-meaning or sacred. Orthodoxy, to the moral anarchist, is a discipline imposed in the name of God that has no relation to God. It is merely a set of established beliefs, not necessarily better than any others, whose acceptance by a person necessarily narrows the realm of his private exercise of choice. In no way should this use of the term "anarchism" be interpreted as denying proper functions of government, as it was used in the thought of Benjamin Tucker or Emma Goldman; nor should the word be interpreted as denying the existence of a universal moral law. The term applies only to the area in which such ideas are explored, accepted, and rejected, not to the ideas themselves. Thus "moral" or "ethical" anarchism implies neither acceptance nor rejection of God or a moral law, or the state, government, or any other idea. It merely holds that unless one is permitted to do wrong, one cannot determine right. Such freedom is necessary for the flourishing of the Remnant, and thus is invaluable to society.

The mode of reasoning behind this theorizing might best be illustrated by repeating the legend of Mithradates VI, called Eupator, greatest of all the kings of ancient Pontus. In the first century B.C., Mithradates succeeded to the throne when his father was murdered. At the age of eleven he was not able to exercise any power in the intrigue-ridden court, and when his mother attempted several times to kill him, he fled to the mountains. When he grew up, he returned, killed his younger brother, and put his mother in jail. After years of often successful forays against the hated Romans, he asked a Greek mercenary to kill him, since poison had no effect on him.

The poison is important. Mithradates is supposed to have been pathologically distrustful of everyone. This is understandable, since most of his ancestors on the throne had been murdered in one fashion or another, and constant attempts were being made on his own life by his closest relatives. So Mithradates, convinced that he was most vulnerable to poison, began making himself immune to it by taking small, gradually increased dosages, until he became so saturated that his own attempt at suicide by poison failed. In other words, by preparing himself for the attacks of the world he survived them, and made himself immune to them. Trusting no one and constantly fortifying himself, he was as independent of others as it was possible to be in the times of Roman imperialism.

The situation is analogous to Nock's moral anarchism. To Nock, the only way to maintain one's integrity was to keep it constantly exposed to the demands of the world, and to improve, as by over-increasing dosage, one's ability to cope with fortune. Within reason, the more men are tried the more they find they can accomplish. The family should make sure that not too much is attempted too soon. Government is instituted solely to maintain optimum conditions for such a life. It has negative functions only, and should not interpose itself between man and his environment. Poison, of itself, is not good, but it exists and it may be administered, and the only way to prevent its being fatal is to make oneself immune by previous exposure.

Thus the true basis for freedom was that it was necessary for moral and spiritual growth and maturity. "The practical reason for freedom, then, is that freedom seems to be the only condition under which any kind of substantial moral fibre can be developed. . . . In suggesting that we try freedom, therefore, the anarchist and individualist has a strictly practical aim. He aims at the production of a race of responsible beings."[13]

One could only do the Right Thing if he had the freedom to do so. One of the things Nock had against America was that people seemed to go out of their way to find things wrong and then tumble about making laws to cure them. This was not the way the problem should be handled. One possible solution was the British way. In Britain, to take an outstanding example, fornication was not a crime. An unmarried couple might set up light housekeeping together and remain undisturbed by the law, "and if anyone else disturbs them the law will protect them; for English law protects those against whom it has no stated grievance, even though their conduct may not be exactly praise-worthy or popular." Should they register at a hotel under differ-ent names, "the law will not only leave them at peace but will protect their peace." English law is concerned only with sex relations concerning children, "to safeguard immaturity," and in the case of adultery, "to safeguard a property-interest, or the vestiges of one." All other liaisons "are put over into the third region of conduct and left subject to the individual sense of the Right Thing."[14]

In other words, if one were to believe that fornication was wrong, he could only do so if he could believe and act otherwise —if he wanted ethical beliefs which had any meaningful foun-dation. Fornication might then be right or wrong, but the law should have nothing to say about it. It might be wrong for some people and right for others, but no one should have the power or right to impose his beliefs on others. This position would not deliver society over into the hands of immoralists—unless it were assumed that the mere exposure to evil was sufficient for corrup-tion, and not, as would appear more likely, a factor in enabling a person to cope with future evil. The concept of "wrong" had no meaning unless the right to be wrong existed and could be exercised without penalty. A person need not indulge, but he must be able to, should he wish to. Only in this fashion could a responsible, realistic morality be developed.

Nock's position, then, was ethical or moral anarchism, a term applying only to the atmosphere of the practicing of belief, and not to a specific belief. A moral anarchist believed necessarily only in the freedom to be wrong, and loathed the doctrine that man was his brother's keeper. Such freedom was necessary for the growth of the Remnant, and because of this it was necessary for the growth of society, since only through the Remnant could social progress be achieved. Like Mithradates, one did not have to like poison to know its dangers and prepare for it.

CHAPTER TEN

THE JEFFERSONIAN AS A CONSERVATIVE:

The Onlooker, 1932–36

"IF the present drift of things continues," Herbert Spencer once wrote, "it may by and by really happen that the Tories will be defenders of liberties which the Liberals, in pursuit of what they think popular welfare, trample under foot."[1] The phenomenon Spencer had noted fifty years earlier suddenly possessed importance for Nock. Against his will, he found himself falling into the arms of the very conservatives he had so vehemently attacked during his first twenty years in public life. Such a movement was not, at first, due to anything but common distaste for the administration. Later, the philosophical tenets of conservatism appealed more and more to him.

The coherent opposition to the New Deal found its first voice in March, 1934. The main objectors were Hoover and the lesser echoes of his brand of conservatism, who repeated the reassuring litanies of faith in decentralization, Americanism, and initiative, and recoiled in horror from the "third rate college professors," petty bureaucrats, and welfare peddlers of the administration. In 1934, Hoover published *The Challenge to Liberty*. During the next three years, Ogden Mills came forth with *What of Tomorrow? Liberalism Fights On*, and *The Seventeenth Million*. Columnists like David Lawrence, Frank Kent, and Mark Sullivan kept up the weekly attacks between books. The New Deal, these writers proclaimed, would inhibit recovery, undermine the qualities of initiative and self-reliance, and lead America to despotism and communism. Most of them advocated a return to the platforms of the 1932 election: balanced budget with reduced government spending, restoration of the gold standard, an end to experimentation, and a stop to government support of labor against capital.

By midsummer, 1934, the conservative Democrats were in revolt. Led by Al Smith, Jouett Shouse, John W. Davis, and John J. Raskob, these men, almost all of them wealthy, met and finally emerged with an organization. They refused to be labeled Republicans—it would have been unfeasible—so they retreated into the American past for their vocabulary and came up with the name of the American Liberty League. Never before having paid much heed to Constitutional limitations unless they proved remunerative, they suddenly began talking learnedly about the Founding Fathers and the liberties they bequeathed. Their economic self-interest and pious fulminating did not impress most observers, even those unenamored of President Roosevelt. "They were deeply moved about the Constitution of the United States," Senator Borah noted acidly. "They had just discovered it."[2]

This opposition was automatic, and of predictably low intellectual content. It had more the character of the "irritable mental gestures which seek to resemble ideas," of which Lionel Trilling has written, than of thoughtful criticism. Such opposition continued throughout the New Deal, with little concrete result. Soon, however, a more effective opposition to the New Deal, a reasoned, non-conservative, intelligent opposition made itself felt. This second opposition was the foundation for the high grade of criticism that developed, primarily on the pages of the *American Mercury*, later in the decade.

II

One of the characteristics of the American political system is that of the left–right conception. Americans have accustomed

themselves to thinking in terms of poles: a right pole beginning
with some form of military or fascist dictatorship; a right center
of conservative thought dedicated to little change, high tariff,
Christian religion, and a mild nationalism; a center favoring mild
social welfare legislation and moderation in all things; a left
center, dedicated to persistence of effort against evils—poverty,
discrimination, ignorance—and usually internationalist in emphasis; and a left pole, unreligious and materialistic, favoring a
totalitarian dictatorship, at worst, a severe socialism at best. The
problem with such a polar conception is that it bears little relation to reality. Some figures fit neatly into the scheme, but many
others do not.

The reasoned opposition to the New Deal did not fit into this
scheme. Most of its members favored free trade, laissez-faire
capitalism, social equality, and an end to privileged exploitation
of government by any special interest. In short, these men were
firmly in the tradition of Thomas Jefferson. They opposed the
New Deal and the Liberty League with equal vehemence, and
found their ancestors in Manchester liberalism and Herbert
Spencer. "The simple truth," Nock wrote in disillusionment, "is
that our businessmen do not want a government that will let
business alone. They want a government they can use. Offer
them one made on Spencer's model, and they would see the
country blow up before they would accept it." Such men were
out for their own profit, not for the good of the country. Nock
had hoped that the depression would teach these men a lesson,
but it did not, and he was disgusted: "This is my first experience
with genuine dyed-in-the-wool Bourbonism, and it has filled me
with such utter disgust that I never want another."[3]

The opening guns of this third force in American political
thought were fired by two dissident Democrats, Lewis Douglas
and James P. Warburg, shortly after the formation of the American Liberty League. They placed themselves firmly in the Jefferson–Spencer camp, and preached the need for local welfare
measures in opposition to both no welfare and federal welfare.

As though to illustrate the difference between these two men and themselves, the Liberty Leaguers began spreading money and propaganda about the country. They even stooped to the level of gallus-snapping Governor Talmadge of Georgia, who was more than glad to have the money.

The Republicans were split between the immovable conservatives, led by Hoover, and the diluted liberals who favored some of the New Deal measures but who placed emphasis on economy and freedom as well. Governor Landon, Colonel Frank Knox, and Senators Vandenburg and Borah were the leaders of this group. Neither group was noticeably Jeffersonian. The eventual candidate, Landon, was little different from the Bull Mooser he had been in 1912. The Jeffersonians were vocal, but without a political base. Virtually all had once been Democrats, few were enthusiastic about Roosevelt, and most attacked him violently. The Republicans, Bull Moose and conservative, offered no solace.

On extremes, further opposition to Roosevelt developed. The socialists and Communists were easily placed on a left–right spectrum, and had a great deal of support. The Popular Front was soon born. Men of the stature of Dewey, Niebuhr, Hook, and Max Eastman were supporting Norman Thomas. But such movements had little political force. Their influence lay in their publications, and their ideas permeated many of the thinkers within New Deal ranks. Then, unclassifiable and incoherent, but providing color, excitement, and oratory enough to move Mencken into rhapsodies of prose, were the splinter groups who united after a fashion behind Lemke: Father Coughlan, Francis Townsend, the remainder of Huey Long's empire, and Gerald L. K. Smith. With a huge audience but primitive organization and confusing statements of policy, these men could not be classified as serious opposition in the intellectual sense. Certainly the inflation schemes of Townsend, the racism of Smith, and the protofascism of Coughlan were hardly within the Jeffersonian framework of the serious and reasoned opposition.[4]

III

During the first years of the New Deal, Nock approached politics in exactly the same way as he had on the *Freeman*. He did not attempt to analyze existing problems; much of the time he was not even in the country. His approach and terminology were based on Oppenheimer. His sympathies were opposed to any political man, party, or cure.

The development of his line of thought was detailed in his journals, which portray the views of a man who could not be identified as Tory, Republican, or any of the other names which supporters of the President attempted to pin on their opponents. Significantly, the single taxers of the *Freeman* days followed a path simliar to Nock's. The position of these people was classified as Jeffersonian, and only by so labeling it could the various strands of opposition to Roosevelt be kept recognizable.

Nock first registered his dislike for Hoover, who, he remarked, "has shown himself all his public life as absolutely nothing but an incarnation of *la bassesse de l'homme interessé*." Hoover was the living embodiment of the ethic of *Fordismus*, a favorite term for the ethic of business America. Hoover, Ford, Coolidge, and the rest were either philistines or barbarians. In Hoover, the effects of *Fordismus* had produced a man devoid of civilization: "I have seldom seen it so pertinacious and at the same time so unrelieved by any offset, in any human character."[5]

Elections were meaningless, for at their best they produced nothing but a change of imposters. Politics, if anything, was even drearier a topic in the thirties than in the twenties. Almost inevitably it corrupted every man who aspired to public office. The American politician was "a sorry figure, driven by the demons of need, greed and vainglory into all kinds of despicable doings, a poor miserable fellow. . . ."[6] Nock had no great and abiding faith in the new President. Perhaps, even probably, he would be better than Hoover, but the inherent evil of political office would corrupt even the good he attempted. Roosevelt "will go only so far, and in such directions, as will further his stay in office, which will of course improve things somewhat; he is expected to sweep clean, but will be careful to sweep no cleaner than he must."[7]

With such opinions, Nock sailed for Europe, and from February 25, 1932, through October 2, 1932, he was traveling through his old haunts in France, Portugal, and Belgium commenting on American politics only when a rare newspaper or relevant letter fell into his hands. When he returned, the importance of politics in the journals increased, and specific issues were more often mentioned. Certainly his distaste for Roosevelt, and even more for Farley and Connolly, grew, confirming all his opinions about politicians. Nothing the administration did during this period was anything more or less than an appeal for votes.

Nock's opinion of Roosevelt as a man—the only way Nock cared to judge a person—was confirmed by an acquaintance: "A man closely associated with Mr. Roosevelt for many years, and quite friendly towards him, has just told me that he never once knew him to make a move, even the slightest, without considering first and foremost its political effect."[8] Roosevelt cared nothing about the condition of the people, and everything about the possession of his job. Even if he had proved to be a disinterested politician, his merit would not necessarily have been greater in Nock's eyes. Roosevelt did not have the qualities of civilization which Nock admired. He was a barbarian, rather than a philistine like Hoover. For practical purposes, the distinction was meaningless.

Opposition also came from a modern American version of the Manichean heresy. In such a view, no middle way exists between light and dark, right or wrong—and usually, the present world is dark and wrong. The classical economic system was right, and the statist conception of man subordinated to a superstate wrong. Like Walter Lippmann in *The Good Society*, and von Hayek and von Mises in later books, Nock held that the New

Deal, whether consciously or not, had moved into the tradition of Fichte and Hegel, the tradition that said that the rights of society were primary, and the source of the rights of the individual: "What ought to be understood, and is not understood, is that Rooseveltism, Hitlerism, Stalinism, are all only local variants of the common doctrine that man has no natural rights but only such as are created for him by the State; the doctrine of State absolutism, formulated by the German idealist philosophers in the early part of the last century."[9]

One trouble with the New Deal was that, like Huckleberry Finn, Nock felt that he had been there before and did not want to go back. His education had acquainted him with the regime of Eubulus in Greece, with the price regulation in China (350 B.C.), state distribution in the first century after Christ, and an R.F.C. plan in the eleventh century. He had no hope that modern schemes would be better. "State monopolies are very old; there were two in China in the seventh century B.C. I suppose there is not a single item on the modern politician's agenda that was not tried and found wanting ages ago."[10]

Another trouble was the mental climate produced by the dole. "The worst of this ever growing cancer of Statism is the moral effect. The country is rich enough to stand its frightful economic wastage for a long time yet, and still prosper, but it is already so poverty-striken in its moral resources that the present drain will quickly run them out." Nock himself was poor, to the point of going into debt to friends. Unlike many other opponents of Roosevelt, he had no economic resources whatever to protect. His opposition originated in this case from the comments of a friend of his. This friend had kept workers at a loss for eight years rather than let them starve, out of compassion and a sense of responsibility. The government, under NRA, had stepped in and tried to tell him how to run his business. He fired his workers forthwith, saying "If the government proposes to tell me how I shall run my business, it can jolly well take the responsibility." Nock commented: "That is the frame of mind that Statism inevitably breeds, and a nation that is in that frame of mind is simply no nation at all. . . ."[11] The incursions of the state bred corruption in both moral and intellectual integrity, a condition fatal to any kind of civilized life. A person dependent on the state for a handout was not his own man. As such he could be nothing but an anthropoid.

Nevertheless, nothing but common hatred of the moment tied Nock to the conservatives at this time. The thought of Hoover writing a book on the challenge to liberty left him speechless with disbelief. His only comment when he found words was to quote Henry Adams to the effect that there was no such thing as an underestimate of average intelligence. He finally realized, however, that Hoover was saying things that were remarkably similar to the economic pronouncements that he himself had been formulating. Herbert Spencer's prediction seemed inexorably to be coming true. "Any one who mentions liberty for the next two years," Nock wrote, "will be supposed to be somehow beholden to the Republican party, just as anyone who mentioned it since 1917 was supposed to be a mouthpiece of the distillers and brewers."[12]

The activities of the dissident Democrats were as unappetizing as those of Hoover: "I see that a Liberty League has been formed, with Jouett Shouse at the helm, and John W. Davis, Nathan Miller, Wadsworth and Al Smith as charter members. *Vilescit origine tali* [It is damned by such an origin]. I have heard of several people as being keen about it, not one of whom I believe to have an honest hair in his head."[13] The Jeffersonians and Georgists had yet to appear, but the first harbingers of enlightenment seemed to augur badly for the opposition to the New Deal.

The elections of 1934 only confirmed first impressions. Roosevelt had bought support and only further debauched the qualities of the voters. "I am not especially indignant at the spectacle of Two-Job Jim Farley buying votes at wholesale, but I am indignant at the sight of people who appear to think it is quite the thing to be done."[14] The whole affair was of course meaningless. Its only consequence was that the Republicans, led by Borah and Theodore Roosevelt, Jr., had found it expedient to copy the

New Deal, since no plums would come their way if they did not. "This means simply that the New Deal is here to stay, as a permanent resource of waste and theft, and that the Republican party is by way of reorganizing to compete for the management of it. In other words, it means that the Republican politicians smell money, and want to garner it in."[15]

Nock made no comments at all on what should be done, if anything, to halt unemployment, only criticisms of what had been done. But he was not attempting anything further. Indeed, the second volume of journals was not even published while he was alive, and was thus hardly to be taken as ammunition in a campaign. Only later did Nock take the administration on with respect to specific measures and suggest alternatives. For the moment, he devoted himself to his "little book on the State," which he had put off so long.

IV

Nock continued his habit of deductive reasoning during the first years of the New Deal, in total methodological opposition to the approach of most contemporary thinkers. He did not look at events and say that something had to be done. He said: Certain things are true, regardless of circumstances, and unless a person pays attention to these, all efforts will come to naught. "When revolutions have cost more than they came to, as has sometimes happened," he wrote in 1932, "it has been for one or more of three reasons. First, they were not directed against the right object; second, they were not run by the right people; third, they did not stop when they were through."[16] In the world of public affairs, proper places existed for men of thought and men of action. Each should be aware of the other and profit from the work of the other. The duty of the men of thought, such as Nock, was to point the way for the men of action.

Our Enemy, the State was Nock's attempt at pointing a way. Published in 1935, it received mixed reviews and had little influence on the course of events. The book, however, could not be dismissed as easily as New Deal thinkers wished. Its value was, first, that it indicated opposition to the New Deal from sources other than the Liberty League or from the Marxists. Second, the book provided a record of how the old single taxers reacted to the forces of statism. Third, it provided a reinterpretation of the Jeffersonian tradition that had long been implicit in Nock's thought. Finally, the book brought Spencerian doctrine into the twentieth century, and emphasized the disparity that had existed between Spencer's politics and the government of the United States.

The book, as a whole, was strongly pessimistic. Nock thought that little could be done to stop the decline of civilization as predicted by Cram, but which had been patented forever as a theory years earlier by Oswald Spengler. He hoped only that some of his Remnant might happen upon the book. Dedicated to producing a reasoned order in the mind of the reader rather than a program of action for the politician, the book offended some readers who wished to know what to do and who cared little for theory. Historically, the book followed Oppenheimer in method and George in economic analysis. It depended on Beard's work on colonial America and a recent work on land speculation by Professor Aaron M. Sakolski. Finally, it appeared to have been influenced by Ortega y Gasset's *The Revolt of the Masses*. In briefest outline, *Our Enemy, the State* was an attempt to apply Oppenheimer's methods to the history of England and America, to show how the American state developed from these sources, and to show how the usual attempts at explanation of the American form of government were erroneous.

Two important distinctions were basic to the argument. The first was that between society and the state, a distinction similar to that which I drew earlier in the discussion of morals. Given a certain number of choices, free choice subject to social censure was one means of exercising power; the other was to have the state make law about which choices could be made. One area could increase its province only at the expense of the other. Three indices existed which enabled someone to measure the degree to which the state had usurped functions from society.

One could look at the "point to which the centralization of state authority had been carried," one could observe "the prodigious extension of the bureaucratic principle," or one could watch "the erection of poverty and mendicancy into a permanent political asset."[17] Whatever redistribution took place was permanent, and any reversal of noticeable magnitude "would be quite unhistorical, quite without precedent, and . . . therefore most unlikely."[18] The New Deal, run by political hacks and second-rate bureaucrats, would stop at nothing to increase its political power. This avarice contributed speed to the redistribution from social power to state power that had been going on throughout the history of the country.

A more important distinction was that between the political means and the economic means: Nock's application of Oppenheimer to Spencer. "As far back as one can follow the run of civilization, it presents two fundamentally different types of political organization. This difference is not one of degree, but of kind."[19] "The State" was historically the organization of the political means. In practice, the term meant all functions of the governing body of a positive nature. "Government" was historically the necessary guardian of the economic means, the safeguard of social power, with only negative functions. "Based on the idea of natural rights, government secures those rights to the individual by strictly negative intervention, making justice costless and easy of access; and beyond that it does not go. The State, on the other hand, both in its genesis and by its primary intention, is purely anti-social."[20] Epstean's law—that man always tends to satisfy his needs with the least possible exertion—meant that the state would always expand at the expense of society, since the state was the organization of the political means and thus required less exertion from its officials than manual labor would have.

The book dealt in detail with the evils of organization and the law of diminishing returns when applied to religious and political history. If freedom was the first affirmation of the book, small size was the second. Only little, loosely organized institutions were controllable. Thus Christianity's worst moment came when Constantine made it into a state-sanctioned institution. Its attractions suddenly included temporal considerations and corrupted whatever good the religion had. Republican England and colonial America were states which only paid lip-service to republican slogans. The earliest settlements in America were commercial states, and from those days "the merchant-State is the only form of the State that ever existed in America."[21] Nowhere in the American colonial experience was there ever a trace of democracy, and "the philosophy of natural rights and popular sovereignty was never once exhibited anywhere in American political practice during the colonial period, from the first settlement in 1607 down to the revolution of 1776."[22]

Some reviewers, probably those who were familiar with the *Freeman* essays and not with Nock's later work, mistakenly supposed that because Nock still quoted Henry George approvingly he was still a single taxer. Nock admired George, and always considered his economics sound. He was not, in 1935, a believer in human perfectibility, the philosophical basis for the single tax. The true affirmation in the book was of the principles of Jeffersonian localism. Not since *Jefferson*, ten years earlier, had the ideal man come in for such extended reference. The organization of the country into wards, the strict interpretation of constitutional powers, and hatred and fear of "the generalizing and concentrating all cares and powers into one body" were especially stressed.

Thus Nock paid particular attention to the Articles of Confederation. Later scholars have upheld Nock's view that the country was not in trouble during this period, and that desire for power and monetary reward were the reasons for the convention that produced the Constitution. These articles set up a state, just as the Constitution later did, but it was a state that was controllable, that could do the least damage to the individual. Only local units could levy taxes. The central government had to live on sufferance and self-granted funds. The federal government could not control because it had no source of revenue it could depend on. Its only real purpose was the conduct of foreign affairs, and these could be minimized if not all but dispensed with. Life under the articles was easy but not ideal. Only life under a government could provide that. These early states levied tariffs, allowed monopolization of land, and were otherwise statist, but their small size kept the possible outrages under control.

The typical review of *Our Enemy, the State* commented favorably on Nock's style and challenged the validity of the distinction between state and government. Others complained about the pessimism of Nock's view that little could be done. Several chided him on the single tax views he had given up—even the sympathetic Isabel Paterson went astray here, despite her affinity for and approval of many of Nock's ideas.

George Soule, in the most intelligent dissent, argued that the state was a necessary evil and that Nock had no real replacement for it. He seemed both attracted and repelled by the book. "Mr. Nock is one of the best essayists and one of the soundest commentators on political history in our times," he wrote. "In a brief book he has managed to distil more shrewd perception of the Puritan and American revolutions than can be found, so far as I know, in any other volume, of whatever length." On the other hand, "if one did not know that he is still alive, one would suppose that he had closed his mind about 1789—or rather, that he had then fallen into a cataleptic trance, interrupted subsequently only by a brief period of lucidity during which he read Henry George."[23] In other words, Nock was being called reactionary. For the first time in his life, he received applause from the conservatives and criticism from the liberals—such as the labels meant, at any rate. He was classified this time not by his friends but by his enemies.

The voice of the conservatives was Seward Collins in the *American Review*. Collins said that although one might quarrel with Nock over the appropriateness of the terms "state" and "government" for the areas in which Nock used them, such a dispute was meaningless because a true dichotomy existed. His

view was typical of the views of non-Marxist critics of Roosevelt: "What a relief to read a really good book on politics! Even
to disagree with Mr. Nock, to the small extent that is necessary,
is a pleasure. His writing is lucid with the lucidity of thought
long ripened in a rich and powerful intellect."[24]

Only Ralph Adams Cram, however, placed the book in its
perspective in twentieth century theory. Hardly a Jeffersonian
himself, the noted architect was still one of the non-conservative,
non-Marxist opponents of the New Deal. In his long and generally favorable review, Cram pointed out the virtues of the colonial
Americans which Nock had purposely not mentioned, while
agreeing with Nock's analysis. To Cram, *Our Enemy, the State*
fitted "elegantly into the significant sequence of revealing volumes that are the white hope of a better day." As such, the book
would have no effect on the mass man, but would act as a means
to right thinking for future societies and theorists. Right thinking
to Cram was as important as it was to Nock; so was Nock's view
of society. Cram, too, felt that the decline of social power was
the reason for the decline of culture and humanity. He and Nock
spoke the same language about the good life. He wrote of the
book's place: "From Spengler on through Ortega y Gasset,
Berdyaeff, Orton, Niebuhr, Agar, Carrel, Dawson, and a dozen
or more providentially of their own kind, we come now to Mr.
Nock, who in a way seems to precipitate theory into fact and in
two hundred sincere pages reveals the sinister visage of the
Enemy of organic Society and hits it a smashing blow."[25]

Smashing it was, perhaps, in theory, but in practice it was
submerged and unnoticed. The book found many appreciative
readers—it has been almost constantly in print for twenty-five
years—but no one crusaded for it and few spoke of it as the
means of a change in their thought. Like Jefferson, it was left to
work its way in the quiet corridors of the mind. In the New Deal,
it seemed a voice from another era, singularly inappropriate in
the minds of those who felt that something had to be done, and
that theory could have little place when men were unemployed
and starving.

CHAPTER ELEVEN

THE JEFFERSONIAN AS A CONSERVATIVE:

The Participant, 1936–39

IN the twenties and thirties, The Players was a center for the off-hours meeting of literary men. Fronting on New York's Grammercy Park, the club had a long and distinguished history. Nock had met a number of his old friends there, among whom was the young, newly appointed editor of the *American Mercury*, Paul Palmer. The two had had a passing acquaintance for some ten years before Palmer became editor and asked his fellow club member to contribute to the magazine. He expressed appreciation for Nock's style, and agreement with the views he had just read in *Our Enemy, the State*. Nock, startled to find someone who was not over sixty years old who liked his work, agreed to write for Palmer, and a strong friendship began, to last until Nock's death in 1945.

With his first *Mercury* article for Palmer in January, 1936, Nock re-entered the world of public affairs. Not since the *Freeman* had he concerned himself for any length of time with current events. The activities of the New Deal and the evident paucity of intelligent opposition, combined with the chance to work with a friendly editor, convinced him to concern himself again. His column, the monthly "State of the Union," covered the whole realm of public affairs, but concentrated on politics. These essays, similar in neither style nor length to his pieces for other magazines, nevertheless revived his interest in a world he was too prone to ignore. Their content was an application of his pessimistic view of history and state action, and the need for culture and civilization in an age of depression, to the daily activities of the Roosevelt administration.

The *Mercury* was the most vigorous opponent of any distinction that the New Deal had. During this period, 1936–39, the political articles were most often written by Nock, Cram, Mencken, Beard, Lawrence Dennis, and Ernest Boyd, a collection of people who agreed on little but their opposition to the administration. Other sections of the magazine were also distinguished. Louis Untermeyer was poetry editor, Ford Madox Ford published monthly literary estimates, Irving Kolodin wrote the music reviews. Other contributors included Fletcher Pratt, Havelock Ellis, G. K. Chesterton, Henry Morton Robinson, Edgar Lee Masters, George Santayana, William Henry Chamberlin, Bertrand Russell, Mark Van Doren, and Agnes Repplier. The editorials, when they appeared, were written by Palmer or Nock. Often they were the product of a conference between the two.

The general policy of the *Mercury* was similar to that of the *Freeman*: if things were to happen, the minds of men must be acquainted with what was true; only then could progress occur. Elections, Nock had written at the very outset of the New Deal, should be "the disposing our people to a better sense of their condition." Since elections in America did not follow Burke's dictum, journals of opinion had to fill the gap. Thus the political and social commentary in the *Mercury* was an attempt to educate, to acquaint people with the sense of their condition. "We are interested only in encouraging our readers to think for themselves, but really to *think*."[1]

In the first article of his regular monthly column, Nock outlined his Jeffersonian third position, as a basis of operation for those neither Marxist nor conservative. The New Deal, he remarked, was nothing more than a continuation of the American belief that government existed to help business. No sharp break had occurred with any tradition in 1933 or later. Coolidge had done his best to use the government to help business, and Roosevelt was doing exactly the same thing. Roosevelt's methods had changed to meet changing times, but the basic belief had not changed. In other words, most Americans wanted government to help only them; this was the "American tradition" of rugged individualism. "Practically no one wants the uniform policy of purely negative intervention. Each would probably be willing enough to see that policy vacated in the case of all the others; but to see it vacated *for him* is simply something that will not bear thinking about."[2]

The New Deal also was a continuation of prohibition. The two phenomena were alike in inception and in professed intention. "As for their fundamental principle, they are so far alike that the one is a mere expansion of the other." Both were brought about as the work of a determined minority working in a time of upheaval. Both wished to do something to America for its own good. Both had laudable desires to eradicate definite evils. Both were enacted when professional politicians saw that votes could be gotten from making pious bows toward the sincere men who actually began the agitation. Both relied on force to achieve their ends. Both could have no more effect than to make corruption and hypocrisy respectable. Just as prohibition did not stop drinking, but rather encouraged it, so the New Deal would not halt pauperization and unemployment, but would encourage them. The two phenomena only weakened social power and increased state power. This was the true crime.

II

Nock and the *Mercury* were opposed to public relief as a matter of principle, but this would hardly account for the utter distaste which they had for the New Deal. Nock, with his disdain for politicians, ignored the chance that Roosevelt and his men might have good intentions and a deep sympathy for men in distress. He also attributed to plan events that were due to merest chance, and he seemed not to realize the essentially im-

provised nature of most New Deal legislation. Instead of accident, he saw malevolence; where good was intended, he saw
only the desire for votes. The quality of man that Roosevelt
seemed to be—an amiable jobholder—was not worthy of admiration, but neither was it grounds for wholesale onslaught.
What caused Nock to see the New Deal as all black was the
mountainous evidence that Roosevelt, and even more, Hopkins
and Farley, were playing politics with human misery. The issue
was less what the New Deal accomplished than it was the kind
of men accomplishing, and their motives. These men, Nock's
indictment ran, never did anything beneficial for the people unless political gain accompanied it. All the agonized fustian about
the underprivileged and the ill-housed, ill-clothed, and ill-fed
was nothing more or less than a smokescreen of liberal preach-
ments designed to cover the greatest attempt in the history of
America to erect an impregnable political machine.

No one denied that the New Deal enabled Democratic politicians to set up such a machine. The argument was that this
was inevitable in the face of great need, that in no other way
could the country survive without terrifying poverty and misery.
Nonsense! said Nock. After outlining the most recent example
of vote-buying (Kentucky primaries, 1938), he wrote that, given
the idea that the government owed its citizens a living, Roosevelt as an honest man could have done two things to prove his
stature as a statesman. He could have "demanded that every
recipient of governmental aid should be disfranchised while
receiving it," or he could have stipulated that "governmental aid
should be confined strictly to supplying the destitute with food,
clothing and shelter, on a system of non-interchangeable vouch-
ers." Thus no one would starve and public money would not be
spent on movie tickets, beer, and tobacco. Such policies were
quite practical, especially when one considered the enormous
popularity Roosevelt had in 1933. When such proposals were
given to the administration, however, it was horrified. "The Administration could not dream of subjecting luckless citizens to
such gratuitous humiliation and obloquy; the mere suggestion

was slanderous, the product of an evil mind." It also would have prevented an enormous political windfall.[3]

The sense of decency was not the only reason for opposing Roosevelt. In the material world, "the irreparable damage which the New Deal has done the country is by its perfection of a political technique entirely new in America." The first step in this technique was "the pauperization of vast numbers of the electorate with public money." People grew accustomed to irresponsible dependence on the state. Why should a man work when he could just as easily, or even more easily, exist on the dole? Such a man did not try to find work, he tried to get a bigger dole. He was valuable only for his vote, and was not his own man.

The second step in the technique was "to raise paupership to the dignity of a recognized and honorable status." Paupers developed an *esprit de corps* about their position as oppressed sufferers in an iniquitous economic system. To such an extreme had sunk the democratic dogma. No longer was the pauper recognized as shameful and disgusting; because a few who would work could not, the whole group of those who were not working was raised to the level of the involuntarily unemployed. All paupers under the New Deal were victims, equally deserving. After all, each man's vote was equal to his companion's.

The third step was "the intensive cultivation of a whole series of group hatreds." One of the classic methods of state action in history was to give the people a bête noire to distract them, and then quickly enact legislation that might otherwise not pass. If people were worked up about the deeds of the very wealthy, anything done by Congress or the President in the name of redressing grievances would be permitted. Likewise any measure to improve racial status could be passed, even if it bore no relation to racial problems, as long as the people thought it did. To set up his political machine, Roosevelt focused public attention on the involuntarily unemployed, and by so distracting attention was able to enact measures that entrenched the Democratic party permanently into American life as a majority party.

The fourth step was "to keep a well-disciplined body of shock troops steadily at work behind an immense smokescreen of humanitarian propaganda." This was but another way of saying that the more people a person fed, the more people a person had voting for him.[4]

Even the material deficiencies of the New Deal were not the whole story. Throughout his public career, Nock had insisted on the idea of the good life as the ultimate end of action, as well as the degree of social power necessary for the individual to attain this. Later, he saw that only through maximum social power could the resources of both the Remnant and the average man be developed to their full extent. Society as a whole depended on the Remnant; the Remnant depended on social power. Thus anything, most specifically state action, which decreased social power was dangerous to society. The New Deal decreased social power to the greatest degree possible.

One sign of this decline of social power was the absence of any of the indignation which had characterized the liberals of the old school. The qualities of Spencer and Bright, of Henry George, Brand Whitlock, and Steffens, of Villard and Randolph Bourne seemed to have disappeared in a sea of subsidized apathy. "Not only his [man's] liberty is gone, but something much more valuable, his belief in liberty and his love of it, his power of quick and effective resentment against any tampering with the principle of liberty by anybody." The qualities not used atrophied, and man was less than he had been. "This is as much as to say that his self-respect, dignity, his sense of what is due to him as a human being, has gone, and that is exactly what I mean to say."[5]

Finally, the humanitarian instinct had been damaged. People were incredulous when Nock remarked that the thing the New Deal had most damaged was the instinct to do the good thing. After all, were not people being fed? The question begged the issue. Herbert Spencer had made a great point of the beneficial aspects of charity, of the benefits to the giver as opposed to the receiver, and a person who did not understand this reference was lost. The instinct of charity and human concern was essential to the civilized man, just as economic security and sound education were. When the state pre-empted the field of charity (and Nock had detailed the sharp reductions which had occurred in the funds to philanthropic organizations in earlier articles), individuals could not cultivate this instinct. The great majority of people, having no idea of what a civilized man was, had no conception of the qualities needed for his growth, and Nock's criticism here was laughed at even by opponents of the New Deal. The state took care of charity, so the common man needed look out only for himself. Only in recent years have some clergymen come forward to point out the essential Christianity behind Nock's outlook. In the thirties, however, it was more blessed to receive than give. If any expression could sum up Nock's position on the New Deal, it would be, "the cure was worse than the disease." From the point of view of civilization, a state which did nothing would have been more beneficial than one which did anything. Poverty was bearable; the loss of any concept of the good life was not.

III

During the depression, Nock wrote two essays showing how one man should act in political office and how a people could avoid things like depressions if only they really wished to do so. The two essays provide a kind of touchstone to Nock's critical commentary on Roosevelt.

William Jay Gaynor, the plain-speaking, Jeffersonian mayor of New York in Nock's days on the *American Magazine*, "was the greatest man, taken all around, that has appeared in our public life since Mr. Jefferson, and also the soundest American." Gaynor did not prostitute himself before the masses, he growled at them. He did not make unctuous noises before minorities, he read them the riot act whenever they trespassed on his idea of the minimum order necessary in a democracy. He was a man of learning, culture, and humor, with a great range of interests and wide learning. Furthermore, in an age of moralists and uplifters led by Anthony Comstock, Gaynor hated "pretentiousness and showmanship, especially when it took the guise of civic virtue."[6]

As an administrator, Gaynor was the ultimate Jeffersonian. To Nock he was guided by five principles, principles that Jefferson, Henry George, and Herbert Spencer would have found admirable. He believed, first, that "ours is a government of laws, and not of men." He believed, secondly, that "the only way to enforce the law is the way prescribed by law." Third, that "no public man or institution is wise enough or good enough to put himself or itself above criticism." Fourth, he believed in common sense in law. Legislation should be held to a minimum: that which was necessary to maintain "outward order and decency," and that which was enforceable. Nothing should be enacted simply because its good was desirable. Fifth, he believed that the office should seek the man, and that the man should be circumspect about listening. Judge Gaynor turned down two gubernatorial nominations, one of which (1910) was considered a stepping-stone to the Democratic presidential nomination which went eventually to Wilson.

Such a man as Gaynor was an anomaly as a politician, and Nock implied that his success was virtually an act of God, so unlikely did it seem. Gaynor was a man who had principles and was true to them, and he was not slow to make them clear to all who would listen. He was a civilized man, a man of humanity. Only such a man could win favor with Nock.

If Gaynor provided the ideal man as politician, the Amish in Pennsylvania provided an example of one kind of ideal society. Nock, of course, was far from endorsing the Amish religion, or many other aspects of their life, but, he pointed out, in 1941 the Amish had yet to discover the depression, and enjoyed life in a society that was secure in the correct sense.

Like Nock in his secular approval of the agrarian life, the Amish held the religious belief "that the agrarian life is the one most in accord with the Scriptures." In pursuance of their faith, they postulated simple doctrines that aimed "at making him [the

Amish man] an upright man and a good farmer." In their religion, they evaded the pernicious effects of size and organization by appropriating no money, building no churches, and allowing all who wished to leave the community. Above all, the community was self-sufficient without force. The Amish man accomplished this fact by being actually "a farmer, not a manufacturer, like our large-scale, single-crop producers. Nor is he a political farmer, of the kind whose perennial sorrows lie so close to the heart of Mr. Wallace." The Amish asked "no political favors from anybody. His produce goes first to feed his family and his livestock." Only then was he interested in cash. Not money or wealth, but self-sufficiency and quality were the goals of the Amish man and his farm.

The Amish program was the best social security possible, the one most in accord with their religion and the Jeffersonian virtues: "When you grow old you simply take things easy, and live *wie Gott in Frankreich* while your family carries on." No "officious nincompoop" from Washington could interfere or debase you by bringing servile dependence. No Amish was ever entered on the relief rolls; none would be. He needed no insurance: "If lightning strikes his barn, his coreligionists in that district build him a new one; if he is ill, they help out with his work; if he dies untimely, they make arrangements to have things go on." Such was the force of social power, if only the will to use it existed and no one interfered.[7]

The point was not that America should turn Amish, but that only by recognizing that man is a land animal in need of the help of others could the necessary social power be generated. Men willing to live only for their own benefit and the benefit of the immediate community could avoid depressions and live useful lives. Men who insisted on the need for great wealth would have to risk great poverty. Men who asked the government to help them in prosperity should not cringe when government forced them to give up their liberties when others achieved political dominance. The Amish attempted only the possible, and only in moderation. By not demanding utopia, they achieved it.

IV

Nock despised labels as intellectual crutches signifying immaturity of thought. "Imposter-terms," he called them, after Bentham's use of the term. But a discussion of his years as a journeyman scholar would not be complete without taking up the labels that, increasingly, were applied to him, and his reaction to them.

"I see I am now rated as a Tory," he wrote Canon Bernard Iddings Bell in 1933. "So are you—ain't it? What an ignorant blatherskite F.D.R. must be! We have been called many bad names, you and I, but that one takes the prize."[8] Nock thought it odd that an announced radical, anarchist, individualist, single taxer, and apostle of Spencer should be called conservative. The names persisted, however, for American voters and publicists seemed to have a constitutional inability to envision any positions other than conservative, middle-of-the-road, and liberal. Nock was thus classified by the enemies of the moment: a conservative in the world of Franklin Roosevelt.

By 1936, the indignation had passed from the term, but remained on those who used it sloppily. Nock became resigned to the portent of the W. S. Gilbert ditty from *Iolanthe*.

> I often think it's comical
> How Nature always does contrive
> That every boy and every gal
> That's born into the world alive
> Is either a little Liber-al
> Or else a little Conserva-tive

His finding himself in the conservative classification was not without justification in at least one area. In education, Nock could be called with a great deal of justice if he had to be called anything, either a conservative or a reactionary—neither term implying correctness, but simply indicating the direction of turning, if a person is to turn at all. His politics, being unclassifiable, were conveniently put into this slot. After all, a man of the mind in the time of Thurman Arnold had certain timeless qualities that hardly seemed modern.

If he had to be labeled, however, he wished to define the label to suit himself. As his model conservative Nock chose Lucius Cary, Viscount Falkland (1610–43). The older Nock grew, the more Cary's outlook appealed to him. Cary's guiding maxim could be set down as a *sine qua non* of conservative thought: "When it is not *necessary* to change it is necessary *not* to change." Thus conservatism was "not a body of opinion, it has not a set platform or creed." It was "purely an *ad hoc* affair, its findings vary with conditions, and are good for this day and train only." It most definitely was not an attitude or sentiment. "Dickens's fine old unintelligent characters who 'kept up the barrier, sir, against modern innovations' were not conservatives. They were sentimental obstructionists, probably also obscurantists, but not conservatives."

Furthermore, conservatism was not the antithesis of Nock's brand of radicalism. "The antithesis of *radical* is *superficial*." Thus a man could be both a conservative and a radical with no contradiction implied. Nock regarded himself as both. So was Falkland. "He was never for a moment caught by the superficial aspect of things." A person could be a great radical and still be extremely conservative about the force of necessity exhibited by a given set of conditions. A radical, in one case, "may think we should get on a great deal better if we had an entirely different system of government," while at the same time "he may take a strongly conservative view of the necessity for pitching out our system, neck and crop, and replacing it with another." The sloppy carpenter could knock the house down even while repairing it. "The conservative is a person who considers very closely every chance, even the longest, of 'throwing out the baby with the bath-water,' as the German proverb puts it, and who determines his conduct accordingly."[9]

So, without especially changing his ideas, Nock moved from

being considered a radical to being considered a conservative. He had disliked heartily the system of government under which Coolidge had operated, yet he felt that Roosevelt's system was worse. He did not advocate revolution but intellect, since only by intellect could a revolution have any good result. He could believe in the single tax without advocating its imposition, since the great upheaval would be too much and the people were unsuited to such an anarchical "government." Because people were not so fitted as to be able to live in George's society, they needed a limited government, based on the economic means and not the political means, along the lines of Spencer's *Social Statics*. When it was not necessary to change, it was necessary not to change, and unplanned revolutions such as the New Deal would inevitably destroy more than they repaired.

v

The years of the journeyman scholar, 1924–39, closed with the publication of *Henry George: An Essay*, and the end of Paul Palmer's reign as editor of the *Mercury*. The new men on the paper, Lawrence Spivak and Eugene Lyons, requested Nock to remain, and out of politeness he continued his column through September. The crusading atmosphere that enveloped the paper offended him, however, and he was glad to leave.

The years had been characterized by certain basic currents. With only one basic doctrinal change, the loss of faith in perfectible humanity, and the resulting tentative adoption of Cram's ideas on great men, Nock nevertheless shifted in the eyes of others from the extreme left to the extreme right. His philosophy, at heart, remained a modern example of the tradition of Jefferson, Spencer, and George, but the ghosts of the pessimists, Henry Adams, Spengler, Ortega y Gasset, cast broad shadows. Here, certainly, was no wide-eyed romantic like the advocate of World Scouting more than twenty-five years previous, but a stoic, a little weary and sometimes despairing, yet not without a confirmed faith that certain things were good and worth fighting for.

Jefferson might never have recognized his admirer, but the changing times had brought changing ideas, and an evolving, and thus healthy tradition.

The last year of the decade, 1939, was a time of upheaval. World War II began the month Nock published his last *Mercury* column. He was sixty-eight, in poor health much of the time, and increasingly isolated because of his political convictions. A few friends, Mencken, Cram, Beard, Palmer, and now Frank Chodorov, were his main contacts with the outside world. More and more he was content to ignore world events and retire to his Canaan Mountain or Rhode Island South County retreats, to enjoy the much-derided simple pleasures which he regarded as basic necessities for the man of culture. He had made his last trip to Europe. His active career was over.

⟋ EPILOGUE–RETIREMENT, 1939-45

No opportunity to talk to the Chief Justice about current troubles until just as I was coming out and then I told him I was very proud of the way the court was handling itself and the way he was handling it. He said, "You must remember we are living in a new world." I said, "I do realize it but it is a world that I do not recognize."

—H. L. Stimson, *Diary,* April 3, 1937

CHAPTER TWELVE

SERENE ON THE ROCK OF PREJUDICE:

Foreign Affairs and the Jewish Controversy; The *Memoirs*

IF the preceding fifteen years had been calm by most stand-ards, they were busy compared to Nock's life from 1939 until his death in 1945. He visited often with Miss Robinson and Miss Wilson, saw the Palmers at regular intervals, and met Mencken on occasion. He kept up a large correspondence with other fig-ures, but rarely left his secluded hideaways for anything but an occasional trip to New York.

To the rest of the world, a war demanded some attention. Nock ignored it disdainfully, as one more sign of the decline of the West. He had predicted, roughly, the course of events as early as 1915, had repeated many of his predictions in the twen-ties, and then watched everything happen as he prophesied. The war was the result of economic jockeying by statist regimes run by the worst sort of politicians. As such, they should be ignored by the civilized man as much as possible.

The war period, 1939–45, marked the nadir of individualistic, Jeffersonian thought in the United States. In the thirties, Nock and his fellow writers were a minority, but a respected and pub-lished one. When war broke out in Europe, space could still be found in the *Atlantic* and *Scribner's Commentator* for his work. After December 7, 1941, not one major magazine could be found to publish a Nock essay, and he stopped writing them. He oc-cupied himself first with his autobiography, and when that was completed, with book reviewing for a sheet started especially for him.

Of all the books published in America during these years, only six could be considered worthy of mention as individualist literature. Only three were by Americans. One of these was Nock's edition of Spencer's long out-of-print *The Man vs. The State*. Rose Wilder Lane wrote *The Discovery of Freedom*, and Isabel Paterson *The God of the Machine*. Friedrich Hayek published his surprise best-seller, *The Road to Serfdom*, a book less extreme than those of Nock and the two women, which covered much the same ground that Walter Lippmann had in his earlier, equally balanced, *The Good Society* (1937). The Austrian economist Ludwig von Mises published *Omnipotent Government*, a critique of all state intervention into the economy. Finally, Nock published his *Memoirs of a Superfluous Man*, the final statement of his position and the high point in his long career.

II

Nock's essays during the period 1939–41 fell into two categories: discussions of current events based on recently published books, and a two-part discussion of the Jewish problem. He repeated his opposition to any state intervention in the economy, to any interference in the foreign affairs of any nation, avoiding entanglements whenever possible, and most often to hypocrisy, especially as practiced by the British propagandists and their supporters in Washington. Throughout the two years, he continually called on Jefferson as a proponent of his views.

Long ago, Nock had recorded his belief that all governments of the kind that ruled the West were evil. He disliked the German government as much as or more than he did the Russian or British governments. Since most people regarded the British as somehow more righteous in their governing than other people, he directed most of his fire toward London. America should not aid Britain, he wrote, because the British were out only for economic gain, and wished to use America to help its buccaneering.

The Germans were evil in their own right, of course, but the affair was no concern of America. America could wipe out the Germans, but would the new world be noticeably better than the old? Nock predicted a new conflict to succeed the second war as the second did the first. A man would be called on to die for freedom, only to find freedom as much in danger when the war was over. Far better to remain aloof, keep Washington weak, and let the world bury itself. The "fear, hatred and hysteria" that the British were whipping up bore suspicious likenesses to 1914–17. How long would it take before America learned?

The publication of Nehru's *Toward Freedom* enabled Nock to state his views cogently. If Britain were so solicitous about democracy, he asked, why the colonies, why the imperialism, why the plain robbery that the British had perpetrated for years in India and Africa? "My notion is that a good many Americans are beginning to be a little fed up with the great American crusade for democracy, liberty, religion, morality, and all that sort of thing, and here is a book which will make them bite each one of those nutmegs a couple of times before they buy them." The British government, he wrote quoting Jefferson, was "the most flagitious which has existed since the days of Philip of Macedon." It was "not only founded in corruption itself, but insinuates the same poison into the bowels of every other, corrupts its councils, nourishes factions, stirs up revolutions, and places its own happiness in formenting civil wars among others, thus rendering itself truly the *hostis humani generis*." The unimpassioned observer wonders what Jefferson would have said about Stalin and Hitler had he lived over a hundred years later; but then, no one of note was demanding a war for the salvation of National Socialism or of Russian Communism by American soldiers. Nock's ultimate position, in cases like these, was to emphasize that "no living American has ever been, or is now, in the slightest danger from any government in the world except his own."[1]

Nock went unheard, however, and Pearl Harbor united most of the country in favor of the war. Nock's last essay appeared in the December issue of *Scribner's Commentator*. The magazine published one more issue, calling for support of the government with high patriotism, and promptly folded. America had re-entered the world with a vengeance, after twenty-two years of timidity.

III

Throughout his life, Nock had an affection for variety. He loved to sample the special atmosphere of obscure places and institutions. He gloried in observing variations of dialect. Nothing could arouse his rage more than a well-meaning attempt to modernize something quaint or historical or to improve something that worked well enough as it was. In travel, at any rate, he had always been a disciple of Lucius Cary.

His views on the values an outsider could get from a foreign culture were expressed at some length in the twenties. "What I wish the Americanizers could see," he had written, "is how much more interesting our whole collective society would be if alien cultures were encouraged to persist. . . . If I were an American-izer my ideal would be to have at least seventy languages, litera-tures, and cultures established side by side all over the land, rooted deep and going strong." Melting pots were fine if *Fordis-mus* were the supreme expression of civilization, but the man of culture needed the stimulation of variety. "My country will be truly civilized on the day when first some citizen of New Haven, stopping off a train at Worcester, absent-mindedly feels in his pocket for his passport."[2]

Only with this idea in mind can a reader properly understand Nock's essays on the Jewish problem. They were strange essays, and stirred up a great deal of controversy, simply because Nock used words the way he had defined them, not the way others defined them. His explanation of the problem also appeared to be quite erroneous.

Nock had an instinctive sympathy for mysticism, most notice-able in his views of immortality, and an occasional interest, if not belief, in the experiments of the spiritualists. His mysticism also influenced his ideas of culture. Races, he thought, should maintain their own culture, in the interest of preventing a deadening uniformity of life. He was convinced, as Frank Chodorov has pointed out, that the real trouble with most Jews was that they "didn't know enough about their own culture." Nock's own view of the Jews was one of appreciation, not discrimination. Indeed, one of his old friends reports that his resignation from The Players, in the summer of 1941, was the result of a misunderstanding of this sort. Nock had nominated a Jewish applicant for membership and the man had not enough friends in the club to get the supporting petitions that the rules required. Nock thought anti-Semitism was behind the rejection and resigned. His belief was false. The Players did not and does not discriminate on racial grounds; but Nock was not to be dissuaded.

"The Jewish Problem in America" appeared in the June and July issues of the 1941 *Atlantic*. It was written, Nock wrote, because a problem definitely existed and yet "no one else is saying anything about it." The essay was intended as an expression of non-Jewish, intelligent, disinterested thought, in an attempt to explore the problem so that others could do something about it. It was a call to thought, not to action. The problem, as Nock saw it, was "that of maintaining a *modus vivendi* between the American Jew and his fellow citizens which is strong enough to stand any shocks of an economic dislocation such as may occur in the years ahead." Father Coughlan and the Bundists had been fomenting racial ill-feeling for some time, and the results of any further serious economic depression might lead to severe racial antagonisms. The present eruptions, he pointed out, had begun with the depression and appeared to be economically motivated. "A general resentment against any minority," he thought, "is always of proletarian or sub-proletarian origin." One wonders if he had examined the vaporings of a Rosenburg, a Gobineau, or a Houston Stewart Chamberlain.

The problem was that the Jews were essentially different from the basic American racial stock. Not inferior, he emphasized, but different. His was a cultural, not a racial, theory. For years no problem had existed because of general prosperity. There had been intermingling but no intermixture. The basic distinction was one of "soul" (read "heritage"): "The Jews regarded us as an Occidental people among whom they had chosen to live, and appreciated whatever merits we were able to show as such; they took us as we were, associated with us in a perfectly free, friendly, and considerate way, with no effort or pretense at Occidentalizing themselves." They were essentially Oriental, while we were Occidental: "We saw them as first-class representatives of an Oriental people with a great history and a great tradition, worthy of all respect and cordial good will, which we unfeignedly gave them." In other words, they had the distinction of possessing a heritage which Nock enjoyed encountering. He found that the distinctly "Jewish Jew" was culturally exciting, and worth preserving. The Jewish heritage was similar to that of the Turks or the Armenians, and quite dissimilar to that of the Italians or the Irish. After several decades, the latter groups would be absorbed without prejudice into American culture; the former groups, never. Had Nock been discussing the Japanese, and the despicable measures the regime in Washington soon planned for their "relocation," people might have understood him better; after all, a man could see the differences there.

Nock went into extensive examples to prove his point. What he meant, he wrote, was that in each group, Oriental and Occidental, "there were great areas of consciousness which the other could not possibly enter upon, let alone explore; therefore, no satisfactory presumptions could be made upon the content of those areas or upon the reactions which the motion of that content might set up." Each member of a given group has unspoken rapport with fellow members that he does not have with a member of the other group.

Above all, Nock feared the effect of the ignorant mass-mind if faced with economic stress. New Deal policies, he was sure, would bring such distress, and he feared the Jew would suffer greatly. He had no solution of the problem. He regarded the

Jews as the continuators of "the world's most august tradition, and possibly also its oldest," and he hoped this heritage could survive.[3]

Nock's views were subject to scathing criticism in subsequent issues of the magazine. He had, evidently, romanticized conditions extremely in his devotion to cultural pluralism. Few Jews thought they were so inscrutably Oriental to other Americans; some thought the problem Nock saw so threatening did not exist. If not an important contribution to racial theory, the essays did underline the high esteem Nock placed on things of the mind.

IV

The concept of superfluity, however, was the dominant theme of the war years. During the twenties and thirties, the idea had bobbed up at regular intervals; eventually, it provided the unifying theme of the *Memoirs*.

Matthew Arnold had written once that the taste for bathos was implanted by nature deep in the soul of man, and that it would govern him until, "perverted by custom or example," he were brought or compelled to "relish the sublime." What bothered Nock was that, in America, there was no "influence that by common consent can exercise just this power of perversion." In other civilizations, this natural taste for bathos, by common consent, had been "severely modified through processes of perversion." In America, however, it had been "glorified, by common consent, into unapproachable dominance." Americans, he continued, "have no Philistine objection to a good thing; on the contrary, they often accept it. But they accept it without exercising any critical faculty upon it, without really knowing that it is good, or knowing what makes it so."[4]

Several years later, he considered the effect which education in his sense of the word would have on a young American. Such a process, he reasoned, would deprive "a young person of one of his most precious possessions, the sense of co-operation with his fellows." The person would have no real place in American society; he would be isolated, lonely. This would happen because education opened up "channels of interest" of which others were unaware, and gave one the idea that "the interest which absorbs his fellows is not worth mortgaging one's whole self, body, mind and spirit, to carry on." Finally, it showed a person "what sort of people one's fellows become," because of their devotion to their own interests. "Education, in a word, leads a person on to ask a great deal more from life than life, as presently organized, is willing to give him; and it begets dissatisfaction with the rewards that life holds out." Education, in other words, "sends him out to shift for himself with a champagne appetite amidst a gin-guzzling society." He would find, in America, "pre-eminently a society, as John Stuart Mill said, in which the test of a great mind is agreeing in the opinions of small minds."[5]

The educated person was thus superfluous to the America of the ethic of *Fordismus*, or *economism*, as Nock later called it. The image he used to explicate this notion was that of "smoking in church." "In every civilization there is a dominant spirit or idea which gives a definite and distinct tone to the whole social life of that civilization. In America, the tone thought proper in church was *Fordismus*. "It determines, almost always positively, and when not positively then negatively by way of reaction, the individual's line of approach to life, establishes his views of life, and prescribes his demands on life." Americans had such an idea, and their idea was distinctly different from the European. An American in Europe was a smoker in church. No matter how pious his pilgrimage, how culture-happy or eager to learn and profit he was, he looked out of place and could be instantly recognized. So was the reciprocal true. The educated European in America was also smoking in church; he was not in tune with the dominant spirit of the country. Such a person was truly a superfluous man.[6]

v

The *Memoirs of a Superfluous Man* was Nock's final book, and without question his best. His style as good as ever, he ranged over the entire course of his philosophical life, commenting serenely on all the topics that had concerned him. Full of the most encrusted prejudices, stated with an air of religious finality, the book was the record of one man's extended love affair with the best that had been thought in four thousand years of recorded history.

Nock had rebelled against the thought of an autobiography for years. He despised the prurient curiosity that seemed to permeate most efforts in the field, and only when William Harlowe Briggs of Harper & Bros. suggested "a history of ideas, the autobiography of a mind in relation to the society in which it found itself," did Nock finally capitulate. He began work in the spring of 1941, and finished two years later.

He told of his "characteristically French" family on his mother's side, with its atmosphere of skepticism and its maxim, "learn to say No." He mentioned, in passing, his brief baseball career. But from a biographical standpoint, the book omitted more than it included. Like Henry Adams, Nock kept his personal life veiled. He did not mention his marriage or his children, or drop the names of all the people he had known. The book described one man's odyssey in search of the good life, and personal details were irrelevant. Again, he told of his views on literature, education, politics, and religion, and of how his three laws, Epstean's, Gresham's and the law of diminishing returns, corrupted much of what was fine in the fields he considered.

Toward the world of war he directed little attention. He believed, with Spencer in 1898, that "we are in the course of rebarbarization, and that there is no respect but that of military despotisms, which we are rapidly approaching."[7] Half of Europe had fulfilled Spencer's prophecy; Nock felt that America would soon follow—he saw no way out. "Things and actions are what they are," Bishop Butler had remarked, "and the consequences of them will be what they will be."[8] The course of statism could not be stopped. Like a severe disease, it would have to run its course; it would get worse before it got better, and very little could be done about it. Like his beloved Spencer, Nock believed and repeated "that there never was, never is, and never shall be, any disorder in nature,"[9] and that one could but sit back and watch the deluge. With Marcus Aurelius, he believed that "in the course of things, those which follow are always aptly fitted to those which have gone before; for this series is not like a mere enumeration of disjointed things, which has only a necessary sequence, but it is a rational connexion." He who sows the wind must reap the whirlwind. "All existing things are arranged together harmoniously, so the things which come into existence exhibit no mere succession, but a certain wonderful relationship."[10]

In a society given over to *Fordismus,* Nock was a superfluous man. Whenever he had been in the United States, he had felt like a smoker in church. America seemed to have no place for a man of the mind, and so he had left often for his refuge in Brussels. "The whole sum of it was that I was like a man who had landed in Greenland with a cargo of straw hats. There was nothing wrong with Greenland or with the hats, and the man might be on the best terms with the Greenlanders in a social way, but there was not the faintest chance of a market for his line of goods."[11]

Politically, the enigma of conservatism, radicalism, liberalism, and so on seemed resolved. Throughout his life, Nock had reversed the usual process. Normally, a person would expect to find, in the story of an intellectual, a man of radical mind but conservative instincts, the kind of person whose mind tells him to be a socialist but whose instinct requires a wife, two children, and a dog in Darien. The history of the last fifty years overflows with men who began as Greenwich Village socialists, anarchists, and free-lovers, and who eventually rejoined their middle class societies. Mark Schorer's *Sinclair Lewis* is only the most recent example of the middle class man whose instincts conquered a rebellious intellect. Nock, however, had radical instincts with a conservative mind. His long training in the Great Tradition had pointed out the follies of thousands of years of great reformers, and much as he wished to believe in reform his mind returned, even in the twenties, to the path of Lucius Cary. He had lost a great deal of innocence with World War I, and he had adopted the ultimate in skepticism with Cram's theory; but never had he been a crusader. Always, forever the true critic, he had worked only in the area of men's minds, never in the field of action. Surely, such predilection is the sign of true conservatism, under whatever label it parades.

The reviews of the *Memoirs* were predictably violent; most were favorable. T. F. Woodlock in *Commonweal*, H. I. Brock in the Sunday *Times*, Isabel Paterson in the *Herald Tribune*, and the anonymous reviewer for *Newsweek* often took exception to specific points, but recommended the book as interesting, well-written, and pleasantly annoying. Clifton Fadiman in the *New Yorker* spoke for these reviewers when he wrote that he had not, "since the days of the early Mencken," found a more eloquent or enjoyable blast against the proprieties. Nock, he wrote, "is a highly civilized man who does not like our civilization and will have no part of it. He is a rare bird, one of an almost extinct species, and, as he very properly puts it, a superfluous one. We are not apt to see his like again."[12]

Orville Prescott, guardian of the morals of his thousands of middle-class female readers, was properly furious. Nock was "steeped in a corrosive, contemptuous cynicism and a profound intellectual despair," and his opinions were "violent, contrary and cantankerous." Nock thought "the worst of most men and their motives" and expected "the worst of all developments and events." His view of the two world wars was "a moral nihilism that is almost criminal. A disillusioned awareness of evil and stupidity does not excuse the complete abandonment of the good fight against them." Nock's views were "not conservatism, or even reactionism," but rather "a denial of life itself." The man was possessed of "a colossal arrogance," and his book "strikes me as one of the vainest, most cocksure, most self-satisfied books in years." Yet even Prescott was struck by the "sinewy, graceful, supple" prose, and despite its idiocies, found it often "interesting and provocative."[13]

But Rolfe Humphries, the distinguished classicist, had the last word in the *New Republic*. A person had occasion to wonder whether he was referring to Prescott when he wrote that Nock's "attitude of mind, it goes without saying, is most provoking to the adolescent, the sentimentalist, who will inevitably pronounce his ideas defeatist, cynical, pessimistic, despairing." This he thought was false. Nock's attitude reminded him rather of Lucius Septimius' question in Shaw's play: "Does Caesar despair?" and the reply: "He who has never hoped can never despair. Caesar, in good or ill fortune, looks his fate in the face." And how, Humphries queried further, "does one reconcile accusations of pessimism and despair with the fact that Mr. Nock writes with such cheer and good grace, such absence of moroseness and gloom?" Nock, he thought, was "a happier man than those who deplore him, or disparage; and again I am reminded of Shaw, and the rebuke of his ancient in 'Back to Methuselah': 'Young man, one moment of the ecstasy of life as I know it would strike you dead.'"

Humphries agreed that Nock was not optimistic about humanity's capacity for improvement, but thought it wrong to say that he was uninterested in methods of reform. Had he not proposed the simple individualist credo that the only thing a person can do to improve society was to "present society with *one improved unit*?"

Fittingly, this review was the last Nock received in his life. To a great degree, Humphries' closing statement was the proper criticism of Nock's whole outlook.

This literary autobiography, then, runs counter to the general rule in more senses than one. It improves as it goes along. Once one gets over the conventional awe of Mr. Nock's formidable reputation, over the apprehension that the writer will turn out to be dogmatic and smug, over the mortification attendant on the discovery that he had read and knows more than you do, then one goes along with increasing interest and delight, marking more pages, and more passages on the page. Before I leave him, I would like to express one trifling dissent from Mr. Nock's judgment. He calls himself a superfluous man, and I know, for he has explained, what he means. But in the cosmic sense—all reviewers are privy to the secrets of the cosmos—he is no such thing. For he is on the side of the angels, who have never yet been known to complain that there were too many on that side.[14]

VI

When he had given the manuscript of the *Memoirs* to Harper, Nock turned again to book reviewing. Because no magazines were interested in the work of anyone who opposed the war, several wealthy friends, working through the National Economic Council, got up a news sheet for him to edit. The first issue of the *Economic Council Review of Books* was dated May 15, 1943. Nock continued as editor and sole reviewer until April, 1945, when he was too ill to continue.

His last two issues have a certain interest for the scholar, for they show first that Jefferson remained a hero to the end, and second, that the Jeffersonian tradition had become a conservative one. War, Nock wrote in March, 1945, was only a means of consolidating and increasing state power—the old liberal position Randolph Bourne had found so basic. Nock claimed to be a true Jeffersonian, in that his attitude came from the man's statement: "Let the heathen rage! Their affairs are not ours, and if they get into a tangle, it is distinctly not our job to straighten them out."[15]

In the next month, he repeated his adherence to the Spencerian program of action. The true conservative would not try to change people, and would not attempt social coercion. He advocated the early liberal policy of "ruthless retrenchment and repeal; the programme of the British Whigs and early Liberals, who saw that sound reform does not lie in making new laws but in repealing old ones."[16] It was quite an achievement to be a liberal, a radical, and a conservative at the same time. Most critics could not make any sense out of it, even if they were not too angry to try.

If one sentence could be found to sum up Nock's individualist outlook—and as such be an enormous simplification—it would be from Voltaire: "Il faut cultiver notre jardin."

VII

The role of critic in the United States is not a popular one. It is not optimistic boosting but pessimistic knocking, and this is not 100 per cent American. The more irritating the critic, the more isolated he becomes, for fewer and fewer people wish to be seen with him. Conformity has become the whipping boy of sociologists and sophomoric gossips everywhere, to the point where one bastion of conformity is the position of a fierce critic of conformity. When confronted with the unbending, armadillo-armored iconoclast, such critics usually run for cover. Often they take refuge in the quantitative measure: surely he who follows a different drummer and who is so alone must be wrong. The thought may be comforting, but not particularly rewarding.

This reaction is unfortunate, for in a country where ritual has been institutionalized into the cocktail party, the pecking order of car makes, and the spraying of deodorant, criticism, too, has become ritualized and often meaningless. The true critic is abrasive, insistent and immovable. He may well be wrong, but that is immaterial. His function is to move people to thought, to a re-examination of their ideas, to—ultimately—that ideological dialogue so necessary for a healthy society. America rarely sees such exchanges, and is the poorer for it. When someone like Nock arrives, unbending, austere, and impossibly erudite, the automatic reaction has been—and remains—withdrawal rather than confrontation.

It is as critic and not as political thinker, of whatever label, that Nock should be remembered. He was far more a gadfly than an expounder of a fixed position. If, as should be obvious by now, he was often wrong, misguided, or simply eccentric, he was unfailingly his own man—incorruptible, unshakably honest. If he was also superfluous, it was both the fault of, and a loss to, the country which uncomprehendingly brought his ire and his intellect to life. The perversity of many of his personal and mental habits only hardened in the face of rejection by those who did not even know they had rejected anything. With his cigarette brightly glowing, he strolled erect and stern through the church which once could claim him. But he had to wander everywhere in this fashion, for people were not so terribly different elsewhere. No matter where he stood, he did not seem to belong. He could only spatter ink on the most outrageous of the world's blemishes, and return to his own garden.

NOTES

1. Nock, *Memoirs of a Superfluous Man*, pp. 59–60. Throughout this chapter I have also relied extensively on information obtained in interviews, letters, and certain unpublished documents. The most valuable of the latter will be cited as "unpublished sketch," an autobiographical fragment written by Nock just before he died, at the request of Paul Palmer, and as "Palmer sketch," a brief unpublished appreciation demonstrating Palmer's feelings about Nock. Copies of both documents are in my possession.

2. Nock, *Memoirs*, p. 2.

3. *Ibid.*, pp. 64, 69, 75, 76–77, 79, 97.

4. *Ibid.*, p. 92.

5. Document in my possession.

6. Van Wyck Brooks, *Days of the Phoenix*, "The Freeman."

7. Unpublished sketch.

8. Brooks, *op. cit.*

9. Interviews, unpublished sketch.

10. The favorable quotations are taken from a letter from Ruth Robinson to me, the unfavorable from a letter written by Samuel A. Nock, of which I have a copy.

11. Letter from Lewis Mumford to me, July 28, 1961, in my possession.

12. Suzanne La Follette, introduction to *Snoring As A Fine Art*, a posthumous collection of Nock essays.

13. Palmer sketch.

14. Frank Chodorov, "Gentle Nock at Our Door," *Faith and Freedom* (February, 1955). Reprint in my possession. The same passage, slightly rephrased, is in his *Out of Step*, p. 148.

15. Sedgwick's comment is printed in Chodorov's newsheet *Analysis* (August, 1946), a Nock memorial edition. Until supplies are exhausted, reprints can be obtained for twenty-five cents from Rev. Edmund Opitz, Foundation for Economic Education, Irvington, N.Y.

2.

1. Charles Forcey, *The Crossroads of Liberalism,* a study of Croly, Weyl, and Lippmann.

2. Merrill Peterson, *The Jefferson Image in the American Mind,* pp. 355–76.

3. Nock, *Jefferson,* p. 190.

4. Letter to Isaac H. Tiffany, April 4, 1819.

5. Letter to François de Marbois, June 14, 1817.

6. Letter to Francis Hopkinson, March 13, 1789.

7. Nock, *Jefferson,* p. 154.

8. Letter to Joseph C. Cabell, February 2, 1816.

9. Letter to Samuel Kercheval, September 5, 1816.

10. See also Louis J. Halle, *Dream and Reality,* Chs. 2–4.

11. Jefferson, *Notes on Virginia,* Query XIX.

12. Letter to John Adams, October 28, 1813.

13. It is the subject of Peterson, *The Jefferson Image in the American Mind.*

3.

1. Henry George, *Progress and Poverty,* p. 200.

2. S. S. McClure, *My Autobiography,* pp. 237–38.

3. Lincoln Steffens, *Autobiography,* pp. 496, 516.

4. Ida Tarbell, *All In The Day's Work,* p. 287.

5. Alfred Kazin, *On Native Grounds,* p. 109.

6. William Allen White, *Autobiography,* pp. 387–88.

7. Tarbell, *op. cit.,* p. 281.

8. Ray Stannard Baker, *American Chronicle,* p. 221.

9. Steffens, *op. cit.,* p. 536.

10. Letter to Ruth Robinson, October 11, 1912.

11. "The West Faces The Land Question," *Century Magazine,* Vol. 73, p. 300.

12. "How We Pay Without Knowing It," *American Magazine* (*AM*), Vol. 71, p. 716.

13. "Taxes Two Sides of the Line," *AM,* Vol. 72, pp. 78–79.

14. John Reed, *The Day In Bohemia*, pp. 25–26.

15. "Taxes Two Sides of the Line," *loc. cit.*, p. 78.

16. "A Community That Pays Its Own Bills," *AM*, Vol. 72, p. 222.

17. "True Canadian Reciprocity," *AM*, Vol. 72, p. 430.

18. "Efficiency and the Highbrow," *AM*, Vol. 75, pp. 48–50.

19. "Brand Whitlock," "Raymond Robbins," "Ernst J. Lederle," "Ralph Whitfield Chandless," "J. J. Pastoriza," "Wild Bill Orr," and "E. F. Schneider." All these were in the "Interesting People" section of the *American Magazine*.

20. "Interesting People," *AM*, Vol. 71, p. 41.

21. "Interesting People," *AM*, Vol. 69, p. 599.

22. Tarbell, *op. cit.*, p. 299.

23. Baker, *op. cit.*, pp. 226–27.

4.

1. "World Scouts," *American Magazine* (*AM*), Vol. 73, p. 276.

2. "Peace, the Aristocrat," *Atlantic*, Vol. CXV, p. 593.

3. See Nock's *Jefferson*, p. 204, in particular, for debt to Beard.

4. "Peace, the Aristocrat," *loc. cit.*, p. 597.

5. Carl Van Doren, *Three Worlds*, p. 113.

6. The position of the first two groups is discussed in Charles Forcey, *The Crossroads of Liberalism*, pp. 234–50.

7. See especially Floyd Dell, *Homecoming*, Ch. 31.

8. O. G. Villard, *Fighting Years*, p. 324.

9. Nock, introduction to Brand Whitlock, *40 Years of It*, p. x.

10. Nock, introduction to anonymous first edition of *How Diplomats Make War*, p. x.

11. Francis Neilson, *How Diplomats Make War*, 5th edition, p. 316.

12. *Loc. cit.*, note 10, pp. ix, xi.

13. Neilson, *op. cit.*, pp. 340, 345, 353, 356.

14. *Ibid.*, pp. 371–72.

15. *Ibid.*, p. 373.

16. "Prohibition in Kansas," *North American Review* (August, 1916), pp. 257–58.

17. "Prohibition and Civilization," *North American Review* (September, 1916), p. 407.

18. *Loc cit.*, note 16, p. 258.

19. The Norwegian system was outlined in detail in *Century* (March, 1917), p. 692.

20. "The staff was rapidly recruited, the first accession after Munsey and McDonald being the brilliant Albert Jay Nock, later the creator and editor of the *Freeman*, the best-written weekly yet to appear in the United States, a publication which thoroughly merited a permanent place in American journalism." Villard, *op. cit.*, p. 350.

21. Nock had written "the public will get from him [Gompers, on his European trip] at his best merely the kind of information that a sturdy partisan drummer, traveling continually in an atmosphere of sheer bagmanism is able to furnish; and with all that the people can do nothing" (Villard, *op. cit.*, p. 354). Lamar summed up the thinking of himself and Burleson in a classic utterance: "You know I am not working in the dark on this censorship thing. I know exactly what I am after. I am after three things and only three things—pro-Germanism, pacifism, and high-browism. I have been watching that paper [the *New Republic*] for months: I haven't got anything on them yet, but I shall one of these days" (Villard, *op. cit.*, p. 357).

5.

1. Matthew Arnold, *Culture and Anarchy*, pp. 6, 45.
2. *Ibid.*, p. 47.
3. *Ibid.*, p. 166.
4. *Ibid.*, p. 108.
5. Herbert Spencer, *Social Statics*, p. 67.
6. *Ibid.*, p. 6.
7. *Ibid.*, p. 37.
8. *Ibid.*, p. 52.
9. *Ibid.*, p. 54.
10. *Ibid.*, p. 62.
11. *Ibid.*, p. 95.
12. *Ibid.*, pp. 186, 195, 218.
13. Henry George, *Progress and Poverty*, p. xxi.
14. *Ibid.*, pp. 5–6.
15. *Ibid.*, p. 136.

16. *Ibid.*, pp. 140, 142, 178.
17. *Ibid.*, p. 186.
18. *Ibid.*, pp. 274, 283, 310.
19. *Ibid.*, p. 334.
20. *Ibid.*, p. 340.
21. *Ibid.*, p. 382.
22. *Ibid.*, p. 406.
23. Franz Oppenheimer, *The State,* pp. iv, xiv, 3, 5.
24. *Ibid.*, pp. 14–15.
25. *Ibid.*, p. 27.

6.

1. Ezra Pound, *Hugh Selwyn Mauberley,* poems 4, 5. From *Personae: The Collected Poems of Ezra Pound.* Copyright 1926, 1954 by Ezra Pound. By permission of New Directions.
2. Harold Stearns, ed., *Civilization in the United States,* pp. vii, 139, 140.
3. All *Freeman* editorials were unsigned. I consulted Mr. B. W. Huebsch, the paper's publisher, and made a list from his set of marked copies of the pieces by Nock.
4. "Our Duty Towards Europe," *Freeman* (*F*), Vol. 7, p. 508.
5. "In The Vein of Intimacy," *Freeman Book,* pp. 33–36.
6. Quoted in "The Leadership of Ideas," *F*, Vol. 5, p. 4.
7. "A Programme of Action," *F*, Vol. 3, p. 101.
8. "An Instructive Controversy," *F*, Vol. 2, p. 344.
9. "Shooting Forbidden," *F*, Vol. 6, p. 580.
10. "The Only Way To Intervene," *F*, Vol. 8, pp. 268–69.
11. "Almost all of it [the book] is lifted straight from the works of my friends Mr. Francis Neilson and Mr. E. D. Morel. . . ." Morel's books were *Ten Years of Secret Diplomacy, Truth and the War,* and *Diplomacy Revealed.*
12. Nock, *The Myth of A Guilty Nation,* p. 5.
13. Harry Elmer Barnes to myself, August 18, 1961.
14. Munroe Smith, *New York Times* (July 16, 1922), p. 4.
15. O. P. Chitwood, *Political Science Quarterly* (December, 1922), p. 692.

16. S. B. Fay, *New Republic* (July 12, 1922).

17. "A Reviewer's Notebook," *F*, Vol. 6, p. 359.

18. "Shadow and Substance," *F*, Vol. 6, p. 148.

19. The editors' affection for the book was evidenced by their offering it as a come-on bonus for new subscriptions.

20. "The State," *F*, Vol. 7, p. 393.

21. *Ibid.*, p. 394.

22. "Anarchist's Progress," *On Doing The Right Thing*, p. 159.

23. C. Brooks and W. K. Wimsatt, *Literary Criticism: A Short History*, p. 436.

24. Quoted, *ibid.*, p. 437.

25. Quoted, *ibid.*, p. 439.

26. Lionel Trilling, *Matthew Arnold*, p. 146.

27. *Ibid.*, p. 147.

28. Quoted, Wimsatt and Brooks, *op. cit.*, p. 447.

29. Trilling, *op. cit.*, p. 188.

30. "The Critic and the Ordinary Man," *F*, Vol. 2, p. 200.

31. "A Study in Literary Temper," *F*, Vol. 2, pp. 464–67.

32. Quoted, *ibid.*

33. "A Study in Literary Criticism," *F*, Vol. 3, pp. 10–12.

34. "In Behalf of Religion," *F*, Vol. 8, p. 389.

35. "A Vain Contention," *F*, Vol. 8, p. 485.

36. Nock, *Memoirs*, p. 295.

37. *Ibid.*

38. *Ibid.*, p. 298.

39. Francis Neilson, "The Story of the *Freeman*," *American Journal of Economics and Sociology*, Vol. 7, No. 1 (October, 1946), p. 52.

40. Although this book is not a biography, several of the preliminary readers have asked me to try to settle one matter of some importance—the Nock–Neilson "quarrel." The matter is unpleasant, and the evidence either vague or contradictory.

When I began this study, I had never heard of Francis Neilson. All of my opinions of him have come from people who knew him and/or Nock, and from his published work. All these impressions have been favorable for the Neilson of the First World War era, and markedly unfavorable for the later Neilson, the one of the quarrel. All my information agrees with the comment of Brand Whitlock to Marshall Sheppey: "Poor Frank! He was so much nicer before he got rich . . ."

(*The Letters of Brand Whitlock*, p. 427). Something in Neilson had changed; whatever it was and why, I will leave to his defenders. The fact remains that those I have encountered in the writing of this study —including several who think very little of Nock—have little regard for the later Neilson.

The quarrel, as it is called, was a one-sided feud which Neilson and his wife carried on, somewhat against their will, against Nock. The best source for their side of the argument is "The Story of the *Freeman*," a document which must be read to be believed. This article, more than anything else, has convinced me that Neilson was something of a crank, and that his opinions are such as to make any scholar wary as to their accuracy. I do not wish to belabor the point, but I find this article to be in execrable taste, based on prejudice and misunderstanding so complete as to approach the sublime. In it, Neilson makes the following "points" against Nock: Nock was a sponge, wheedling money and then not paying it back, and an ingrate (pp. 15 ff); he acted in bad faith with Villard over the *Nation*; he was deficient in his knowledge of Matthew Arnold; he loved Rabelais for the obscenity and not the educational passages; he was silent when people discussed foreign and ancient literatures; he was mentally and physically unstable (pp. 18, 21, 22–23, 33–35). Some of these remarks might seem picky and irrelevant, but they are only a prelude. Neilson goes on to accuse Nock of stealing his ideas (pp. 26–33), of shallowness (p. 39), of not sitting properly in a chair (p. 35), and so on. Neilson also narrates several little games which he and his wife indulged in, at Nock's expense, to expose his ignorance. The tone of the piece would be disreputable if written by a teen-age girl who read only movie romances.

The quarrel has two bases. Neilson said Nock claimed, in effect, that Nock did more of the work on the *Freeman* than he actually did. Neilson also claimed that Nock declared that he was co-author of *How Diplomats Make War*. Neilson based all his charges on rumors that he heard, and never anywhere did he quote a word showing that Nock ever claimed either distinction. As Neilson knew perfectly well before he let his temper get the better of him, Nock actually disclaimed both assertions in print (see the introduction to the first edition of *How Diplomats Make War* and Nock's description of the *Freeman* in his *Memoirs*).

What started Neilson fuming was a report in *Who's Who in Amer-*

ica (1933) in which Nock was listed as co-author of his book. Nock, however, never sent a word to *Who's Who*, as he implies in his *Journal of These Days* (Morrow edition, p. 40), as Frank Chodorov suggests in his *Out of Step*, and, most of all, as Nock explicitly says in letters now held by his sons. Nock refused to answer the *Who's Who* questionnaire, and when he found they were going to print something on him anyway, he even went to a lawyer to see if he could sue to make them ignore him. The error was made by the publication, not by Nock. Neilson's case, then, is only that Nock did not deny rumors —rumors which he might never have heard (he was in Europe for most of the period, for one thing). Neilson never understood his old partner anyway, but surely only the most obtuse could fail to realize Nock's supreme contempt for matters of this sort. He would have denied nothing even if he had heard, for he simply could not be bothered about such trivia. It says something about Neilson that he could be so bothered. Neilson could only hypothesize that Nock said nothing because of unpaid debts—the less said about this remark the better.

Anyway, the mistake once made, every reference book compounded it. As late as 1950, *Who Was Who, 1943–50*, claimed that Nock wrote half of *How Diplomats Make War*. The caliber of this "reference" work may be indicated by its statement of Nock's address as "St. Stephen's College, 16 Grammercy Park, New York." That, I would suggest, might give pause to those who thought the school's name was Bard, and that it was located in Annandale, New York. A quick check of other reference works shows that all faithfully copied these errors—an indication of sloppiness on the part of certain compilers.

Nock, for his part, predictably remained silent, and so the Neilson–Nock quarrel never had a second party. Neilson chose not to publish his remarks until Nock died, so of course no refutation could be made by Nock himself. Those of us who have bad posture, who do not relish conversations about obscure Latin poets, and who prefer silence to pointless controversy can only hope that enough has been made of a misunderstanding.

41. Mumford letter (my possession).
42. *Nation* (February 6, 1924), p. 131.

7.

1. John M. Reed, *The Day in Bohemia*, p. 22.

2. Sedgwick to Nock, February 26, 1930. (Copy held by Nock brothers.)

3. "The Purpose of Biography," *Snoring as a Fine Art*, p. 119.

4. "Artemus Ward's America," *Free Speech*, p. 87.

5. "Artemus Ward's America" (1934), "Artemus Ward" (1924), and "Artemus Ward As Critic" (1921).

6. "Artemus Ward's America," *loc. cit.*, p. 92.

7. *Ibid.*, p. 24.

8. "Artemus Ward," introduction to *Selected Works of Artemus Ward*, p. 13.

9. *Ibid.*, p. 24.

10. Nock to Mrs. Evans, *Letters from Albert Jay Nock*, F. W. Garrison, ed., p. 20.

11. M. D. Peterson, *The Jefferson Image in the American Mind*, pp. 405–14.

12. Peterson's introduction to Nock's *Jefferson*, p. vii.

13. Nock, *Jefferson*, p. 203.

14. *Ibid.*, pp. 115, 116.

15. Stuart Sherman, *The Main Stream*, p. 32.

16. S. E. Morison, *New Republic* (December 15, 1926).

17. C. G. Bowers, New York *World* (June 27, 1926).

18. Nock, *Jefferson*, pp. 20, 54, 178, 194.

19. *Ibid.*, p. 51.

20. *Ibid.*, p. 54.

21. *Ibid.*, p. 163.

22. *Ibid.*, p. 67.

23. *Ibid.*, p. 157.

24. Quoted, *Ibid.*, p. 64.

25. Quoted, *ibid.*, p. 66.

26. *Ibid.*, p. 64.

27. *Ibid.*, p. 121.

28. *Ibid.*, p. 161.

29. *Ibid.*, p. 122.

30. *Ibid.*, p. 123.

31. *Ibid.*, p. 190.

32. *Ibid.*, p. 184.

33. *Ibid.*, p. 200.

34. Nock and C. R. Wilson, *Francis Rabelais, The Man and His Work*, p. xxi.

35. *Ibid.*

36. Eliseo Vivas, *Nation* (February 26, 1930), p. 251.

37. B. R. Redman, "Books," New York *Herald Tribune* (December 22, 1929), p. 3.

38. Nock and Wilson, *op. cit.*, p. 162.

39. *Ibid.*, pp. 245, 267–69.

40. *Ibid.*, pp. 84–85.

41. P. 6. "Pantagruelism" was never printed except in the memorial edition of Frank Chodorov's *Analysis*. Numbers refer to pages in that edition.

42. Nock, *Journal of Forgotten Days*, p. 18.

43. *Analysis*, p. 6.

44. Van Wyck Brooks, *Days of the Phoenix*, p. 58.

45. Nock, *Journey Into Rabelais's France*, pp. 21, 49, 297.

46. "Henry George: Unorthodox American," *Snoring as a Fine Art*, p. 86.

47. *Ibid.*, p. 86.

48. *Ibid.*, pp. 86–87.

49. *Memoirs*, p. 128 n.

50. *Henry George*, pp. 153–54.

8.

1. *Journal of These Days*, September 10, 1932.

2. R. A. Cram, *Convictions and Controversies*, pp. 145–46.

3. *Ibid.*, p. 140.

4. *Ibid.*, pp. 148–49.

5. "Isaiah's Job," *Free Speech*, pp. 249–50.

6. *Ibid.*, pp. 255–56.

7. *Ibid.*, pp. 257–58.

8. *Memoirs*, pp. 132–33.

9. *Ibid.*, pp. 133–34.

10. "The Classicist's Opportunity," *Freeman Book*, pp. 52–53.

11. *Memoirs*, p. 270.

12. *Ibid.*, p. 279.

13. *The Theory of Education in the United States*, Regnery edition, p. 44.

14. *Ibid.*

15. *Ibid.*, pp. 47–48.

16. *Ibid.*, p. 50.

17. *Ibid.*, pp. 39–40.

18. *Ibid.*, pp. 50–51.

19. *Ibid.*, pp. 54–55.

20. *Ibid.*, pp. 62–63.

21. *Ibid.*, pp. 65–66.

22. *Ibid.*, pp. 115–16.

23. *Ibid.*, p. 122.

24. *Ibid.*, p. 123.

25. *Ibid.*, pp. 123–24.

26. F. W. Garrison, ed., *Letters from Albert Jay Nock*, p. 68.

27. "The Path to the River," *Free Speech*, p. 340.

28. *Theory of Education in the United States*, pp. 150–53.

29. John Dewey, *New Republic* (April 13, 1932), pp. 242–44.

30. Abraham Flexner, *Nation* (February 17, 1932), p. 207.

9.

1. Thomas Beer, *The Mauve Decade*, pp. 24–25.

2. To Ruth Robinson, June 18, 1913, *Selected Letters of Albert Jay Nock*, F. J. Nock, ed., p. 34.

3. *Ibid.*, June 28, 1913, p. 36.

4. *Ibid.*, to Sedgwick, July 14, 1917, pp. 88-91.

5. "A Word to Women," *Free Speech and Plain Language*, p. 11.

6. *Ibid.*, p. 16.

7. *Ibid.*, p. 19.

8. Unpublished sketch (see note 1, Chapter 1).

9. "Women and the Marriage Market," *Free Speech*, p. 51.

10. *On Doing the Right Thing*, pp. 166–67.

11. Herbert Spencer, "Overlegislation," *The Man vs. the State*.

12. *On Doing the Right Thing*, p. 173.
13. *Ibid.*, p. 174.
14. *Ibid.*, p. 170.

10.

1. Herbert Spencer, "The New Toryism," *The Man vs. The State.*
2. A. M. Schlesinger, Jr., *The Coming of the New Deal*, pp. 471–88.
3. To Ellen Windsor, August 22, 1938, *Letters*, F. W. Garrison, ed., p. 105.
4. A. M. Schlesinger, Jr., *The Politics of Upheaval*, pp. 15–207, 515–570.
5. *Journal of These Days*, October 7, 1932.
6. *Ibid.*, May 11, 1933.
7. *Ibid.*, March 6, 1933.
8. *Ibid.*, December 16, 1933.
9. *Journal of Forgotten Days*, July 21, 1934.
10. *Journal of These Days*, September 25, 1933.
11. *Journal of Forgotten Days*, May 28, 1934.
12. *Ibid.*, July 31, 1934.
13. *Ibid.*, August 24, 1934.
14. *Ibid.*, November 10, 1934.
15. *Ibid.*, December 6, 1934.
16. "If We Must Have A Revolution," *American Mercury* (September, 1932), p. 75.
17. *Our Enemy, The State*, pp. 10, 12, 14.
18. *Ibid.*, p. 16.
19. *Ibid.*, p. 35.
20. *Ibid.*, p. 49.
21. *Ibid.*, p. 92.
22. *Ibid.*, pp. 102–3.
23. George Soule, *Saturday Review of Literature* (January 11, 1936), p. 6.
24. Seward Collins, *American Review* (November, 1935).
25. R. A. Cram, "The Enemy of Society," *American Mercury* (May, 1936), p. 112.

11.

1. Editorial, October, 1938, p. 130.

2. "Progress Toward Collectivism," *American Mercury* (February, 1936), p. 173.

3. "WPA—The Modern Tammany," *American Mercury* (October, 1938).

4. "Report On America, II," *ibid.*, pp. 129–35.

5. "The New Deal and Prohibition," *American Mercury* (March, 1936), p. 33.

6. "Notes On A Great American," *American Mercury* (December, 1932), p. 445.

7. "Utopia in Pennsylvania: The Amish," *Snoring as a Fine Art*, pp. 29–42.

8. To B. I. Bell, December 4, 1933. (Copy held by Nock brothers.)

9. "To Little Conserva-tive," *Atlantic* (October, 1936), pp. 481–89.

12.

1. "Toward Freedom," *Scribner's Commentator* (August, 1941), pp. 90–91.

2. "Post-Marked Dresden," *Harper's* (June, 1927), p. 314.

3. "The Jewish Problem in America," *Atlantic* (June, 1941), pp. 699–706 and (July, 1941), pp. 68–76.

4. "A Cultural Forecast," *On Doing the Right Thing*, pp. 77–82.

5. "The Disadvantages of Being Educated," *Free Speech and Plain Language*, pp. 209–25.

6. "On the Practice of Smoking in Church," *Harper's* (February, 1930), p. 316.

7. Quoted, *Memoirs*, p. 115.

8. Quoted, *ibid.*, p. 152.

9. *Ibid.*, p. 238.

10. Quoted, *ibid.*

11. *Ibid.*, pp. 144–45.

12. Clifton Fadiman, *New Yorker* (September 25, 1943), p. 60.

13. Orville Prescott, *New York Times* (September 22, 1943), p. 27.

14. Rolfe Humphries, *New Republic* (October 25, 1943), pp. 595–96.

15. *Economic Council Review of Books* (March, 1945), p. 4.

16. *Ibid.* (April, 1945), p. 3.

BIBLIOGRAPHY

Aaron, Daniel, *Men of Good Hope*. New York: Oxford University Press, 1961.

Arnold, Matthew, *Culture and Anarchy*. New York: Cambridge University Press, 1960.

Arnold, Thurman, *The Folklore of Capitalism*. New Haven: Yale University Press, 1961.

Baker, Ray Stannard, *American Chronicle*. New York: Charles Scribner's Sons, 1945.

Barker, Charles A., *Henry George*. New York: Oxford University Press, 1955.

Barzun, Jacques, *The House of the Intellect*. New York: Harper & Row, Publishers, 1959.

Beard, Charles A., *The Rise of American Civilization*. New York: The Macmillan Company, 1930.

Beard, Charles A. and Mary R. Beard, *America in Midpassage*. New York: The Macmillan Company, 1939.

Beer, Thomas, *Hanna, Crane, and the Mauve Decade*. New York: Alfred A. Knopf, Inc., 1941.

Bell, B. I., *The Crisis in Education*. New York: McGraw-Hill Book Co., Inc., 1949.

———, *God is Not Dead*. New York: Harper & Row, Publishers, 1945.

Bestor, Arthur E., *The Restoration of Learning*. New York: Alfred A. Knopf, Inc., 1955.

Brooks, Van Wyck, *Days of the Phoenix*. New York: E. P. Dutton & Co., Inc., 1957.

Broun, Heywood and Margaret Leech, *Anthony Comstock*. New York: A. & C. Boni, 1927.

Chamberlain, John, *The American Stakes*. New York: Carrick & Evans, 1940.

———, *Farewell to Reform*. New York: Liveright Publishing Corp., 1932.

Childs, M. and J. Reston, *Walter Lippmann and His Times*. New York: Harcourt, Brace & World, Inc., 1959.

Chodorov, Frank, *Out of Step*. New York: The Devin-Adair Co., 1962.

Colum, Mary, *Life and Dream*. Garden City, N.Y.: Doubleday & Company, Inc., 1947.

Cram, R. A., *Convictions and Controversies*. Boston: Marshall Jones, 1935.

————, *My Life in Architecture*. Boston: Little, Brown and Company, 1936.

————, *The Nemesis of Mediocrity*. Boston: Marshall Jones, 1917.

Current, Richard N., *Secretary Stimson, a Study in Statecraft*. New Brunswick, N.J.: Rutgers University Press, 1954.

Dell, Floyd, *Homecoming*. New York: Farrar, Straus & Co., Inc., 1933.

Ellis, Elmer, *Mr. Dooley's America*. New York: Alfred A. Knopf, Inc., 1941.

Filler, Louis, *Crusaders for American Liberalism*. New York: The Crowell-Collier Publishing Co., 1963.

Forcey, Charles, *The Crossroads of Liberalism*. New York: Oxford University Press, 1961.

Forgue, Guy J., ed., *Letters of H. L. Mencken*. New York: Alfred A. Knopf, Inc., 1961.

Gabriel, R. H., *The Course of American Democratic Thought*. New York: The Ronald Press Company, 1956.

Garrison, F. W., ed., *Letters from Albert Jay Nock*. Caldwell, Ida.: The Caxton Printers, Ltd., 1949.

George, Henry, *Progress and Poverty*, Classics Club edition. Roslyn, N.Y.: Walter J. Black, Inc., 1943.

Goldman, E. F., *Rendezvous with Destiny*. New York: Vintage Books, 1958.

Halle, Louis J., *Dream and Reality*. New York: Harper & Row, Publishers, 1959.

Hicks, Granville, *John Reed, the Making of a Revolutionary*. New York: The Macmillan Company, 1936.

Hoffman, F. J., *The Twenties*. New York: The Viking Press, 1955.

Hofstadter, Richard, *The Age of Reform*. New York: Vintage Books, 1961.

————, *The American Political Tradition*. New York: Vintage Books, 1956.

——, *Social Darwinism in American Thought*. Boston: Beacon Press, 1958.

Huebsch, B. W., ed., *The Freeman Book*. New York: Huebsch, 1924.

Hutchins, R. M., *The Higher Learning in America*. New Haven: Yale University Press, 1962.

Johnson, Walter, ed., *Selected Letters of William Allen White, 1899–1943*. New York: Holt, Rinehart & Winston, Inc., 1947.

Kazin, Alfred, *On Native Grounds*. New York: Reynal & Company, Inc., 1942.

Kempton, Murray, *Part of Our Time*. New York: Simon & Schuster, Inc., 1955.

Kirk, Russell, *The Conservative Mind*. Chicago: Henry Regnery Company, 1960.

Koch, A. and William Peden, *The Life and Selected Writings of Thomas Jefferson*. New York: Modern Library, Inc., 1944.

La Follette, Robert M., *La Follette's Autobiography*. Madison, Wis.: University of Wisconsin Press, 1960.

Lane, Rose Wilder, *The Discovery of Freedom*. New York: The John Day Company, Inc., 1943.

Lippmann, Walter, *The Good Society*. New York: Grosset & Dunlap, Inc., 1943.

McClure, S. S., *My Autobiography*. London: John Murray, 1914.

Madison, C. A., *Critics and Crusaders*. New York: Frederick Ungar Publishing Co., Inc., 1959.

Marshall, J., "The Anti-Semitic Problem in America," *Atlantic Monthly* (August, 1941), 144-49.

Martin, James J., *Men Against the State*. DeKalb, Ill.: Adrian Allen Associates, 1953.

Millet, F. B., *Contemporary American Authors*. New York: Harcourt, Brace & World, Inc., 1940.

Morison, E. E., *Turmoil and Tradition*. Boston: Houghton Mifflin Company, 1960.

Neilson, Francis, *How Diplomats Make War*. Appleton, Wis.: C. C. Nelson, 1940.

——, *My Life in Two Worlds*. Appleton, Wis.: C. C. Nelson, 1952.

——, "The Story of the *Freeman*," *American Journal of Economics and Sociology*, supplement (October, 1946).

Nock, Albert Jay, *Book of Journeyman*. New York: Publishers of the *New Freeman*, 1930.

————, *Free Speech and Plain Language*. New York: William Morrow & Co., Inc. 1937.

————, *Henry George: An Essay*. New York: William Morrow & Co., Inc., 1939.

————, *Jefferson*. New York: Hill & Wang, Inc., 1960.

————, *Journal of Forgotten Days*. Chicago: Henry Regnery Company, 1948.

————, *Journal of These Days*, London: Heinemann, 1934.

————, *A Journey into Rabelais's France*. New York: William Morrow & Co., Inc., 1934.

————, ed., *The Man vs. the State*, by Herbert Spencer. Caldwell, Ida.: The Caxton Printers, Ltd., 1940.

————, *Memoirs of a Superfluous Man*. New York: Harper & Row, Publishers, 1943; Chicago: Henry Regnery Company, 1964.

————, *Myth of a Guilty Nation*. New York: Huebsch, 1922.

————, *On Doing the Right Thing*. New York: Harper & Row, Publishers, 1928.

————, *Our Enemy, the State*. New York: William Morrow & Co., Inc., 1935.

————, ed., *Selected Works of Artemus Ward*. New York: A. & C. Boni, 1924.

————, *The Theory of Education in the United States*. New York: Harcourt, Brace & World, Inc., 1932. Chicago: Henry Regnery Company, 1949.

Nock, Albert Jay and C. R. Wilson, *Francis Rabelais*. New York: Harcourt, Brace & World, Inc., 1931.

Nock, Francis Jay, ed., *Selected Letters of Albert Jay Nock*. Caldwell, Ida.: The Caxton Printers, Ltd., 1962.

Oppenheimer, Franz, *The State*. New York: Huebsch, 1922.

Peterson, Isabel, *The God of the Machine*. New York: G. P. Putnam's Sons, 1943.

Peterson, M. D., *The Jefferson Image in the American Mind*. New York: Oxford University Press, 1960.

Pound, Ezra, "Hugh Selwyn Mauberley." See Hoffman, *The Twenties*.

Reed, John, *The Day in Bohemia, or, Life Among the Artists*. Privately printed in Riverside, Conn., 1913.

Rosenfeld, P., *Men Seen*. New York: The Dial Press, Inc., 1925.

Rossiter, Clinton, *Conservatism in America*, revised edition. New York: Vintage Books, 1963.

Rudolph, F., "The American Liberty League, 1934–1940," *American Historical Review* (October, 1950).

Schlesinger, A. M., Jr., *The Coming of the New Deal*. Boston: Houghton Mifflin Company, 1959.

———, *The Politics of Upheaval*. Boston: Houghton Mifflin Company, 1960.

Schorer, Mark, *Sinclair Lewis: An American Life*. New York: McGraw-Hill Book Co., Inc., 1961.

Seitz, D. C., *Artemus Ward*. New York: Harper & Row, Publishers, 1919.

Sherman, Stuart P., *The Main Stream*. New York: Charles Scribner's Sons, 1927.

Smith, Mortimer, *And Madly Teach*. Chicago: Henry Regnery Company, 1949.

———, *The Diminished Mind*. Chicago: Henry Regnery Company, 1954.

———, *William Jay Gaynor, Mayor of New York*. Chicago: Henry Regnery Company, 1951.

Spencer, Herbert, *The Man vs. the State*. See Nock, ed.

———, *Social Statics*. New York: Robert Schalkenbach, 1954.

Stearns, H., *America and the Young Intellectual*. New York: Doubleday & Company, Inc., 1921.

———, ed., *Civilization in the United States*. New York: Harcourt, Brace & World, Inc., 1922.

———, *The Street I Know*. New York: Lee Furman, 1935.

Steffens, L., *The Autobiography of Lincoln Steffens*. New York: Harcourt, Brace & World, Inc., 1931.

Stimson, H. L. and McG. Bundy, *On Active Service in Peace and War*. New York: Harper & Row, Publishers, 1948.

Tarbell, Ida, *All in the Day's Work*. New York: The Macmillan Company, 1939.

Trilling, Lionel, *The Liberal Imagination*. Garden City, N.Y.: Doubleday Anchor Books, 1953.

———, *Matthew Arnold*. New York: Meridian Books, Inc., 1955.

Turner, Susan, "A Short History of the *Freeman*, a Magazine of the Early Twenties, with Particular Attention to the Literary Criticism," unpublished Ph.D. dissertation, Columbia University.

Van Doren, Carl, *Three Worlds*. New York: Harper & Row, Publishers, 1936.

Villard, O. G., *Fighting Years*. New York: Harcourt, Brace & World, Inc., 1939.

White, Morton, *Social Thought in America*. Boston: Beacon Press, 1959.

White, W. A., *The Autobiography of William A. White*. New York: The Macmillan Company, 1946.

Whitlock, Brand, *40 Years of It*. New York: Appleton-Century-Crofts, Inc., 1914.

————, *The Journal of Brand Whitlock, The Letters of Brand Whitlock*, Allan Nevins, ed. (two volumes). New York: Appleton-Century-Crofts, Inc., 1936.

Wiltse, C. M., *The Jefferson Tradition in American Democracy*. Chapel Hill: The University of North Carolina Press, 1935.

Wimsatt, William K. and C. Brooks, *Literary Criticism, A Short History*. New York: Alfred A. Knopf, Inc., 1957.

Wolfskill, G., *The Revolt of the Conservatives*. Boston: Houghton Mifflin Company, 1962.

American Magazine
    1910: Brand Whitlock (March).
            Cost of Living (June).
            What a Few Men Did in Pittsburgh (September).
            Raymond Robbins (November).
            The Things That Are Caesar's (December, and monthly
                through August, 1911).
    1912: World Scouts, A New Movement (January).
            A New Science and Its Findings: Discoveries by Karl Pear-
                son (March).
            Ernst J. Lederle (August).
            Earning Power of Population (November).
            Ralph Whitfield Chandless (December).
    1913: Is It True? (January).
            J. J. Pastoriza (January).
            What We All Stand For (February).
            A Puritan Heart (pseud. Cav. A. de Angelis) (March).
            Efficiency and the Highbrow (March).
            E. F. Schneider (September).
            Wild Bill Orr (October).
    1914: An Adventure in Education (April).
School Review
    1908: The Value to Clergymen of Training in Classics (June).
Outlook
    1914: Railways and the people (May 2).
            Socialism in Milwaukee (July 11).
Collier's
    1912: Premium on Tax Lying (January 15).
    1915: Jamaica (April 10).

Nation

    1918: Alarming Coal Situation (August 3).

           What American Labor Does Not See (August 24).

           Idle Waterways (October 5).

North American Review

    1916: Prohibition in Kansas (August).

           Prohibition and Civilization (September).

Century

    1917: Should We Fight for Prohibition (March).

           The West Faces the Land Question (December).

    1928: Streets (September).

Virginia Quarterly Review

    1932: Return of the Patriots (April).

    1933: What Are Elections For? (January).

Review of Reviews

    1927: Divorce Market (November).

New Republic

    1932: As Simple as That (January 13).

Bookman

    1929: The Absurdity of Teaching English (April).

Menorah Journal

    1928: More Scraps of Paper (February).

New York Evening Post

    1918: Democracy Here and Abroad (January 30).

Atlantic Monthly

    1914: Motherhood and the State (August).

    1915: Peace, the Aristocrat (May).

    1932: What Every Woman Ought to Know (March).

    1936: Little Conserva-tive (October).

    1937: Letter from the Tropics (April).

           Bright Isle (May).

           Oxometer (September).

    1938: Letters from a Dutch Uncle (May).

    1939: On Hearing Good Music Done Badly (July).

    1940: In Defense of the Individual (June).

           Country Bug (August).

    1941: Second Empire (January).

           Jewish Problem in America (June–July).

Harper's
　1926: Notes of an Emigré (July–August).
　1927: Fists across the Sea (February).
　　　　American Tourist in Europe (May).
　1928: Peace by Incantation (May).
　1929: Mr. Smith and Mr. Smythe (May).
　　　　Officialism and Lawlessness (December).
　1930: On the Practice of Smoking in Church (February).
　1933: Are All Men Human? (January).
Saturday Review of Literature
　1930: Mr. Thomas Jefferson (January 11).
　　　　If Not, Then Not (May 24).
　1931: Lincoln Steffens (May 9).
　　　　One of the Immortals (May 23).
Scribner's Commentator and *Scribner's*
　1932: European Morals and Our Own (October).
　1941: Unfinished Victory (April).
　　　　Union Now (May).
　　　　Out of the Night (June).
　　　　Churchmen and the War (July).
　　　　Toward Freedom (August).
　　　　Getting Us into War (September).
　　　　Prophet at Home (October).
　　　　You Can't Do Business with Hitler (November).
　　　　Review of National Socialism (December).
Economic Council Review of Books, 1934–5
Encore (November, 1944)
Analysis
　1945: About a Book or Two (July).
Atlantic Bookshelf: occasional reviews.

Freeman, 1920–24.

　Volume I
　　　1. The Railways, p. 4.
　　　2. In the Vein of Intimacy, p. 52.
　　　3. The Recognized Irish Republic, p. 76.
　　　4. The Long and Strong Purse, p. 77.

American Mercury

Segregation For Utopians (June).
The Politicians Take Over (July).
The Social Security Fad (August).
Keeping Our Shirts On (September).
Victory By Retreat (October).
The State Can Do No Wrong (November).
The Politician's Opinion of You (December).

1937: Coating the Pill With Hooey (January).
Bogus Era of Good Feeling (February).
The Case For Free Speech (March).
High Cost of Dying (April).
The Autocrat vs. The Constitution (May).
A Government of Men (June).
All The Traffic Will Bear (July).
Liberals Never Learn (August).
Autopsy on the New Deal (September).
The Packing of Hugo Black (October).
The Difficulty of Thinking (November).
A New Dose of British Propaganda (December).

1938: What the Republicans Won't Do (January).
Stealing Tammany's Stuff (February).
Taxing Production To Death (March).
When Is A Murderer? (April).
Government by Racketeers (May).
Down The Rat-Hole (June).
No More Rabbits in the Hat (July).
The Amazing Liberal Mind (August).
Job-Holder's Paradise (September).
WPA—The Modern Tammany (October).
Business Dodges The Truth (November).
Wanted: Honest Radicals (December).

1939: What Is Democracy? (January).
College Is No Place To Get An Education (February).
The Criminality of the State (March).
Culture Migrates To the U.S.A. (April).
Liberalism Has Sold Out (May).
College Men and the State (June).
The Triumph of the Gadget (July).
America's Too Public Libraries (August).
Postscript On the Royal Visit (September).